T0339241

THE
BIG MAN OF
JIM
BEAM

BOOKER NOE AND THE NUMBER ONE BOURBON IN THE WORLD

JIM KOKORIS

WILEY

Cover image: [BOOKER NOE] © Bean Suntory [DRINK] © GETTY IMAGES /
THOMAS WINZ
Cover design: Paul McCarthy

Published by John Wiley & Sons, Inc., Hoboken, New Jersey.
Published simultaneously in Canada.

Limit of Liability/Disclaimer of Warranty: While the publisher and author have used their best
efforts in preparing this book, they make no representations or warranties with respect to the
accuracy or completeness of the contents of this book and specifically disclaim any implied
warranties of merchantability or fitness for a particular purpose. No warranty may be created or
extended by sales representatives or written sales materials. The advice and strategies contained
herein may not be suitable for your situation. You should consult with a professional where
appropriate. Neither the publisher nor the author shall be liable for damages arising herefrom.

For general information about our other products and services, please contact our Customer Care
Department within the United States at (800) 762-2974, outside the United States at (317) 572-
3993 or fax (317) 572-4002.

Wiley publishes in a variety of print and electronic formats and by print-on-demand. Some
material included with standard print versions of this book may not be included in e-books or in
print-on-demand. If this book refers to media such as a CD or DVD that is not included in the
version you purchased, you may download this material at http://booksupport.wiley.com. For more
information about Wiley products, visit www.wiley.com.

Library of Congress Cataloging-in-Publication Data:

Names: Kokoris, Jim, author.
Title: The big man of Jim Beam : Booker Noe and the number one bourbon in the
    world / Jim Kokoris.
Description: Hoboken : Wiley, 2016. | Includes index.
Identifiers: LCCN 2016031585| ISBN 9781119320159 (hardback) | ISBN
    9781119320005 (epub) | ISBN 9781119320173 (ePDF)
Subjects: LCSH: James B. Beam Distilling Company--History. | Noe, Fred. |
    Beam, James B., 1864-1947--Family. | Distillers--United States--Biography. |
    Whiskey industry--United States--History. | BISAC: BUSINESS & ECONOMICS
    / General.
Classification: LCC HD9395.U47 K65 2016 | DDC 338.7/66352092 [B] --dc23 LC record
available at https://lccn.loc.gov/2016031585

Printed in the United States of America.

10 9 8 7 6 5 4 3 2 1

CONTENTS

iii

FOREWORD

My dad, Booker Noe, was an original—that is one thing I am certain of. There weren't any others like him. Opinionated, stubborn, fun loving, smart, curious, and charismatic, he lived life all out. Every day was an adventure. Every day offered another opportunity to explore or try something different. Every day offered another chance to have fun, share a joke, hear and tell another story, meet and make another friend.

Booker had a lot of interests—fishing, hunting, dancing, and cooking—but he really had only one true passion: making whiskey. Very few people do what they were absolutely meant to do—and my father was one of them. He was born to be a distiller, had it in his blood, and took his craft about as seriously as you can. Making whiskey wasn't a job to him, it was a calling. Something he had to do, and something he wanted to do well.

He was more than just a distiller, however. He was an innovator, a big thinker. He liked to tinker, test boundaries, ask what if. "By God, let's give that a try," was one of his favorite expressions. Some of his ideas fell flat; many others succeeded. Success or failure didn't matter as much to Booker as trying did. *Can't accomplish nothin' if you don't try.* If there's one thing I learned from him, it was probably that.

My dad touched a lot of people during his life. Hundreds, if not thousands, called him a good friend. When he met you, he made you feel special. After talking to him awhile, you wanted to be in his orbit, spend more time with him. When Booker was around, everything was pretty much all right or would be soon.

My dad passed away too soon. There were more stories to tell, more adventures to go on, more bourbon to sip. But I'm grateful for the time I had with him.

Booker's gone, but this book, written by my longtime friend Jim Kokoris, brings him back. For those of you who knew him, it will be fun reminiscing and going over old times. For those of you who didn't, well then, fasten your seat belts, you're in for quite a ride.

My best,
Frederick Booker Noe III

PROLOGUE
BOOKER NOE: THE BIG
MAN OF BOURBON

When I-65 South hits Lebanon Junction, it's pretty much a straight shot west to the distillery. A few miles past open fields and woods, and you're there. While other distilleries have enjoyed a renewal in appearance and upkeep, fueled by a relentless bourbon boom, this plant, smack dab in the middle of nowhere, is nondescript, plain. No trolleys, restaurants, gift shops, or historical recreations drawing tourist attention and dollars. Just a handful of gray rack houses and low-slung, cinder-brick buildings set back from the road with a solitary sign marking its presence. If you aren't looking for the place, you could miss it, a dusty and remote outpost, there and gone.

There's little to indicate that this distillery, located on the outskirts of tiny Boston, Kentucky, about an hour south of Louisville, was ground zero for the great renaissance the bourbon industry is enjoying now. But it was. A lot took place here a long time ago, because a long time ago Booker Noe worked here.

Faraway from the inquisitive eyes of marketing executives and tourists, this sixth-generation Beam, a giant of a man both literally and figuratively, was free to ruminate, experiment, concoct, and create. What he ended up eventually doing here changed not only the trajectory of his family's centuries-old company, but the future of the entire bourbon industry as well.

Nowadays the distillery is as busy as ever, pushing out close to 70,000 gallons a day, six days a week. A quick walk around confirms growth: trucks full of grain whiz by, the smell of sweet cooking mash fills the air, and a new barrel recovery system is being built, which will ultimately help produce more whiskey. Bourbon is on fire, especially Beam products, with demand threatening to outstrip supply. And this growth doesn't show any signs of abating.

There aren't many photos of Booker at the plant, no statues or plaques to speak of. All of those are over at the flagship Clermont plant, six miles away in Bullitt County. The Boston distillery does bear his name, though: it's called the Booker Noe Plant, and that would have been good enough for Booker.

It's more than fitting that this place in north-central Kentucky was where Booker Noe—master distiller, grandson of Jim Beam, scientist, artist, raconteur, American Original, and Big Man of Bourbon—spent most of his career. Because, like this distillery, Booker was no frills, straightforward. You get what you see. All Booker Noe ever really wanted to do was make bourbon, and that's all this plant does.

CHAPTER 1

Boyhood

S pringfield, Kentucky, is a fine small town. Picturesque. Clean. A quaint and familiar air of Mayberry-Americana covers the place like a comfortable patchwork quilt. It's about five or six blocks long, with a solid downtown offering sturdy brick buildings, including an opera house, the Washington County municipal building, and a handful of churches. It has some history too: Abraham Lincoln's father and mother were born nearby, a fact duly noted by well-placed historical markers. A cluster of unassuming frame houses presses hard along Main Street a few feet from the road. It was in one of these houses that Frederick Booker Noe II spent his childhood.

Born to Margaret and Frederick Booker Noe in 1929 on December 7 (a day that would later be infamous), Booker was the second of four children. The fact that his mother was the daughter of Jim Beam, the prominent bourbon distiller, didn't mean all that much to the people of Springfield. Even though Jim had made a name for himself in the whiskey business and was known and respected throughout the Commonwealth of Kentucky, the Noes were like every other family in Springfield: a tight-knit clan trying to get through the hard times brought on by the Great Depression. Besides, Prohibition was in force— Granddaddy Jim owned a rock quarry now, not a distillery—and the Beam name didn't have quite the cachet that it used to. Booker's father, known as Pinkie to his friends, was a vice president at the local First People's Bank, and his wife, Margaret, stayed at home to raise the kids and run things.

Being a Beam and the oldest grandson of America's best-known whiskey maker didn't seem to matter much to young Booker either. He was happy being a kid in Kentucky, embracing everything his surroundings could offer. Springfield was primarily a farming town, surrounded by rolling fields of wheat, corn, and tobacco, and Booker and his friends spent their free time fishing the ponds and streams and playing with slingshot guns up at the cemetery that overlooked the town. On Sunday afternoons, after mass at St. Dominic's, where he was an altar boy, Booker would head over to the 100-seat local movie theater with his best friend and cousin Bob Noe Hayden to watch the latest Western. Gene Autry was up there singing and shooting and the boys ate it up. As they saw it, their lives weren't that all much different from those of the cowboys. In their eyes Springfield was a frontier town surrounded by the wild and teeming with adventure—and maybe even danger.

Like most of the country, Kentucky was struggling during the thirties. The Depression hit farmers and the coal industry hard, but the Noes weathered the storm. Pinkie managed to keep his job at the bank, and the family—unlike others in the area—stayed afloat, neither rich nor poor. There were cheese sandwiches for lunch, baloney sandwiches after school, and Margaret's famous fried chicken and mashed potatoes on Sunday. Pinkie's weekend trips to Lexington for University of Kentucky games were also a ritual, as were short family excursions to visit friends and family in Old Green, a green Pontiac that ate up miles like Booker ate chicken legs.

There was also Booker's hunting. When he was 13 he graduated from slingshots to his father's shotgun, and the boy mastered it quickly, taking deadly aim at whatever he could. "When you went hunting with him, you never let him shoot first," his younger brother Jerry recalled. "Because if you did, you wouldn't have anything to shoot at. Whatever he shot at went down and you'd be standing there with your gun in your hand and nothing left to do."

Weekends were spent tramping over fields in search of rabbits, pigeons, and ducks. The boys usually ate what they shot, taking home their kills and cleaning them at the kitchen table. One Sunday morning Booker and a schoolmate trespassed on a horse farm that bordered the Noes' land. Booker had been warned to stay off the farmer's land many times—warnings that had gone unheeded. When the farmer saw Booker standing on top of a hill on this particular day, he had had enough. Grabbing his rifle, he took a shot at the young teen and grazed his pant leg. Booker stayed clear of the farm from then on. There were plenty of other places to shoot ducks.

While life seemed relatively bucolic for the Noes, 25 miles away in Bardstown, Jim Beam was scrambling, confronted by an unprecedented double whammy—Prohibition and the Depression. His distillery in Clermont, which he had bought in 1922, had remained dormant for years, a dilapidated and fading relic. While some of its rack houses still contained barrels of his family's whiskey, federal law prohibited him from selling any, a fact that irked, frustrated, and saddened him. He was a distiller, and distillers make and sell whiskey.

Prohibition had decimated not only the booming Beam enterprise, but the entire bourbon industry as well. At its onset, there had been 17 distilleries operating in the Bardstown area alone. Most of them were successful family-run enterprises, turning out whiskey for a growing and appreciative audience. Almost overnight those plants closed, the doors to their rack houses padlocked forever. A fair amount of the remaining whiskey was bootlegged out, the dwindling supply more precious than ever. The Bardstown area, because its location was central to the various distilleries, became a hub of whiskey contraband. Bootleggers used it as a base of operations, loading and dividing up the liquid, then gunning the engines of their tricked-out cars and trucks before racing out of town on dark back roads to points unknown.

The pockets of a lot of local distillers—and of some local sheriffs—got fat during those times. Envelopes full of cash were offered in return for looking the other way when the whiskey was being loaded up. Some bootleggers didn't bother with cash. They showed up at a warehouse late at night, flashed a shotgun at the watchman, then took what they wanted.

Moonshining became common in the foothills and hollers, with the 'shiners making what they could with whatever ingredients they had. The result was whiskey of dubious quality.

Still, it was a living and families had to get by. So Mason jars were filled.

Jim Beam had chances to sell off his remaining stock, but he opted not to. While he did take a few barrels back to Bardstown, the rest stayed under lock and key back at the plant. Old Jim was a prudent man, and he thought running whiskey wasn't worth the risk. As he told his wife, Mary, "Bourbon ain't worth going to jail for—and besides, Prohibition is going to end soon and before we know it we'll be back in business and all will be right in the world."

So while his whiskey quietly evaporated, floating out through the cracks and holes in the white oak barrels, and while other distillers shut down and walked away, Jim tried his hand at a number of businesses, all of which failed. One of his final enterprises was a rock quarry that backed up to a shuttered distillery in Clermont, about 25 miles south of Louisville. Believing that Prohibition wouldn't or couldn't last long, Jim bought the closed distillery and bided his time while operating the quarry. Even with the help of his brother Park and his nephew Carl, that too struggled. Jim Beam, the fourth-generation distiller and part of a bourbon-making family dynasty, couldn't buy a break—and as a result almost went broke waiting for the blessed repeal.

To be sure, Jim felt the weight of the family dynasty on his shoulders. He was fourth in a family line whose name was synonymous with bourbon. Some 130 years before, his great grandfather Jacob Beam, a pioneer of German descent, had come from Maryland with his young wife, Mary, in tow and passed through the Cumberland Gap. He was looking for a fresh start and new horizons, and he found both at a place called

Hardin's Creek in Washington County, near what would one day be Springfield. It was there that Jacob started a farm, raising hogs and cattle and growing tobacco. He also grew corn because the climate was conducive to it—so conducive that he soon had too much of it. So using a water-driven mill to grind the corn and a pot still he had brought with him from Maryland he began to make whiskey, experimenting with various combinations of rye, barley, and of course, corn, the main ingredient, until he had it right. Soon his whiskey was in demand. Other farmers and travelers made it a point to stop by his farm with an empty jug, which Jacob was only too happy to fill, sometimes in exchange for a nickel, sometimes in exchange for a smoked ham or beaver pelt. Soon whiskey making was his primary occupation and the farm just a sideline, and the name Beam began to spread throughout the Ohio River Valley.

Jacob eventually turned operations over to his son David, who handed things over to his son David M. in 1853. Each contributed his own talent to the business; each moved the business forward. David figured out how to ship whiskey on flatboats to New Orleans, and David M. moved the distillery to nearby Nelson County, close to the new railroad.

Proximity to the railroad was key. Trains, now equipped with steam engines, gave the Beams a fast way to ship their whiskey. The telegraph helped business, too; when barkeeps ran low on liquor, they finally had a way to reach distillers and order more. Also adding to the growth of the industry was a change in the distillery process. David M. and other distillers began getting away from the pot still and using something called a column still. These new stills increased production so that more bourbon could be made.

Thanks to trains and new production methods, bourbon became firmly established in the Ohio River Valley and beyond. It soon emerged as the drink of choice in the Old West. When cowboys bellied up to bars in Dodge City and Austin and other frontier towns and asked for a whiskey, chances are that they got bourbon. It was the drink of cowboys.

During the Civil War, troops on both the Union and Confederate sides had their share of bourbon. In addition to helping to ease pain and fortify a soldier's spirits, it served as an anesthetic to help the wounded. Kentucky was a border state. It stayed in the Union—Mary Todd Lincoln, the wife of the president, was from Kentucky—but you could still own slaves, so it was essentially neutral. Legend has it that when the Union troops came to the Beam distillery, David M. flew the American flag; when the Confederates marched in, up went the rebel colors. Both were good customers.

After the war, David M. launched a new product called Old Tub, which proved quite popular for years. He also increased production. The Beam enterprise was on solid footing when Jim Beam, David M.'s son, joined the business at age 16. Young Jim proved a fast learner, and aided his father on both the distilling and business end. By the time he was 30 he was in charge, and he moved things forward as fast as he could. He built more rack houses to store more whiskey and he hired more people to do more work.

This went on for years. Then Prohibition hit—and it hit hard. Even though Jim had seen it coming (the temperance movement had been growing for a long time), he didn't have much of a plan B. When the law was finally repealed, Jim and his family dusted themselves off and got the old distillery in

Clermont operational as fast as they could. But making whiskey takes time—years—so while Jim's whiskey was sitting in barrels aging, trying to get old fast, thirsty Americans turned to Scotch and Canadian spirits, which were already available and ready for immediate consumption. While Jim's ancestors had, no doubt, faced their own share of problems, they had never faced the challenges that confronted him, and consequently he feared that he might be the last of a line of bourbon makers, a dynasty stopped dead in its tracks.

Booker and his family were somewhat impervious to the problems of Granddaddy Jim. They were one step removed from the whiskey industry. Booker's father never joined the family business, opting instead for the steady paycheck the First People's Bank offered. Still, they remained close to the bourbon-making side of the family, frequently piling into Old Green and heading over to Bardstown to pay Jim a visit. Despite circumstances, Jim and Mary Beam still lived in a house that, while not palatial, was certainly substantive. With its wide front porch and white column pillars it was a fixture on what was called Distiller's Row on North Third Street. The house was across the street from Jack Beam's house (Jim's uncle, who ran the Early Times distillery), and right next door to the home of the Samuels, another renowned bourbon family. There were big Sunday dinners, with bridge games in the parlor and sips of bourbon and water for the menfolk in the backyard on summer evenings. Jim wore a coat and tie most everywhere, and while his collar might have been a little frayed, he kept up appearances just fine.

He also kept a keen eye on his oldest grandson as he watched him run about the yard tossing a football, amazed at his dexterity as well as his burgeoning size. Booker was growing faster than a weed—tall and wide—fueled by an appetite that could only be described as prodigious. Ham, baloney, cheese, bread, pies, cakes, chicken, and fish: no one could eat like Booker. No one.

Booker's weight become more than a curiosity, however, when after a routine check of the boy's tonsils a doctor informed Margaret that Booker was simply growing too big, too fast.

"That boy eats like the man he'll never grow up to be," he told Margaret. "He needs to slow down or he'll never make it to 20."

Try as she might, Margaret couldn't get Booker to ease up at the table. The result was a man-child, a giant who kept eating and growing, his appetite for all things insatiable.

Booker's largeness defined him. Years later he would say, "I'm big, so I've always stood out." He was the largest child in grammar school and later in high school, and because of his sheer size he was literally and figuratively looked up to as a leader, someone to follow. Over time, his personality caught up to his size. He knew people were looking at him and knew he intimidated folks and, while never soliciting that attention, he gradually accepted it and the responsibility that went with it. He became outgoing and popular, generous to a fault, and a fixture at parties and community events. Even as a youth, nothing ever happened until Booker Noe got there.

Despite his build, he wasn't a lumbering giant. Far from it. He was quick on his feet, moving about with an athlete's grace and stamina. He didn't get winded. Rather, even as a boy he could outwork grown men. Consequently he was in demand as a field hand around Springfield, cutting tobacco, beating the seeds out of hemp, bailing hay. Farmers were willing to pay top dollar for the strong Noe boy, who could work 10 hours without breaking a sweat as long as you fed him.

When Booker reached adolescence he went to the local school, Springfield High, but that didn't work out as planned. It seems he couldn't contain his rambunctiousness: His appetite for fun had become as large as his appetite for country ham. He loved parties, especially family parties, where he was known to sneak out and retrieve empty bottles of 100-proof Old Tub from behind the shed and, according to an *Esquire* magazine interview he gave many years later, drink the little drops left in the corners of the bottle. He didn't like what he tasted (hot and nasty), but that would soon change.

Things came to head one day when Booker got ahold of some dead chickens from a local brood house (a brood house is where young chickens that are ready to be sold are kept) and stuffed them in his pocket. The next day he and his friend Bubba pelted his fellow classmates with the chickens while they were on their way to recess. Soon after the dead chicken incident, seeing where things were headed, Pinkie and Margaret decided to ship Booker off to St. Joe's Prep, a boarding school in Bardstown a stone's throw from Granddaddy Jim's house.

It was at St. Joe's that Booker developed a sense of discipline. The school was full of rules, and Booker—the chicken-throwing, corner-drinking cowboy from Springfield—was forced to comply. He was up at 6 AM for mass, which was followed by a quick (and, as far as Booker was concerned, unsatisfactory) breakfast, then six hours of classes, then sports. Students could only leave the campus on Sunday afternoons, and even then just for a short while, to maybe catch a Western at the local theater. After that it was back to the dorm for homework and chores.

Despite the fact that he attended the school with a number of his friends from Springfield, and despite being less than an hour from his parents, Booker was homesick. He missed the freedom of home, the unlimited hunting and fishing, the open fields and rolling hills, and, of course, his mother's cooking. As far as he was concerned St. Joe's was something to tolerate, something to get through until the next thing.

Fortunately, he did have sports. Most of the other boys were from the Bardstown area, but a fair number were from around the country: a handful even hailing from faraway New York City. Almost all were good athletes. As a result, St. Joe's fielded powerhouse teams, especially in football. Booker, because of his size and quickness, excelled and played both as a punishing defensive end and as an impenetrable guard on offense. No one in Central Kentucky wanted to line up against Hard Times, a nickname given to Booker because of his birth date of December 7, by then a day of infamy, and the fact that he was born in 1929, on the cusp of the Depression.

On holidays or when school was not in session Booker would spend time at his granddaddy's house on North Third Street, a few minutes from school. In addition to enjoying home-cooked meals (a needed respite from the dreary food at St. Joe's), Booker would occasionally join Jim on trips to the distillery. They traveled down the two-lane highway in Jim's Cadillac: Granddaddy talking bourbon and Booker listening. Booker wasn't particularly interested in the mechanics of the bourbon-making process—he was only a teenager and the chemistry was beyond him (what exactly is fermentation again?)—but he made an effort to pick up what he could and asked questions when appropriate. He held his reserved grandfather in high regard: Jim Beam was one of the few people who intimidated Booker, and he showed as much respect as he could whenever he was around him.

On their trips Jim emphasized the importance of yeast and Kentucky's fabled limestone-filtered water, two ingredients that made the family's whiskey special. Jim held Kentucky water in such high regard that he would sometimes stop on the way to the distillery and march off into the woods until he found a clear stream where he could fill a jug or two for drinking later. This water is as good as it gets, he told Booker.

These occasional visits to the distillery were the first real exposures Booker had to the family business, and when he got there he liked what he saw. Majestic black-roofed rack houses rising in the early morning mist, trucks full of grain, hard-working Kentucky men talking sports and women, bubbling yeast mats, and, of course, the still blowing off steam. Standing on the front porch of the distiller's house up on the hill where his older cousin Carl and his family lived, he could pretty much take in the whole distillery and see the various parts working together all at once. It seemed pretty interesting to young Booker Noe.

What the boy couldn't accurately see from that porch was the state of the family business. It was the 1940s, and while the U.S. economy was on the verge of the great post-war expansion, the Beam business, like most bourbon makers, was still shaking and sputtering like an old pickup going uphill. The popularity of and demand for Scotch and Canadian whiskey, along with gin, was showing no sign of slowing. As a result the bourbon industry was contracting, with once-prosperous distilleries, such as George T. Stagg and James E. Pepper, selling out to larger enterprises. The future of bourbon didn't look all that promising.

While Beam's main products at the time, Old Tub and Colonel James B. Beam, were fairly well established and gaining awareness nationwide, the business needed an infusion of cash, so the distillery was sold to the Blums, a family from Chicago. Harry Blum had already been a significant shareholder, but his family now owned the whole enterprise: the Beams had relinquished control after close to 150 years. Rather than feeling defeated, the family felt liberated. The business end of things had never appealed all that much to the Beams and the sale freed the family up to do what they did best: make bourbon whiskey. Booker's chance, though it was still a while off, was coming.

Kentucky Limestone Water

The water that Jim Beam liked to fill his jugs with is different, special because it is filtered through an underground shelf of limestone that can be found throughout Kentucky. This limestone water has a high pH, which promotes fermentation. It also adds minerals, such as calcium, and filters out impurities, such as iron. The abundance of this unique water was critical to the pioneer distillers who recognized its value early on and used it to perfect their whiskey.

On the surface, Booker and his grandfather, James Beauregard Beam, shared few personality traits. While Booker was outgoing, the proverbial life of the party who was comfortable in work pants and a cowboy hat, by most accounts Beam was coat-and-tie reserved; a man who saw things in black and white and was a quiet and steady presence at the distillery and family gatherings. In addition to a bloodline, they did share two traits, though: a talent for making bourbon whiskey and a willingness to experiment and innovate.

Born August 25, 1864, in Bardstown, Jim Beam was one of eight children, the third son of distiller David M. Beam. By the time he joined the family business, Beam bourbon, particularly the Old Tub produced by D. M. Beam & Company, was already fairly well established in Kentucky and the Deep South, with a reputation as fine sipping whiskey. With young Jim's help, the company's growth accelerated as critical new eastern markets, such as New York City and Philadelphia, became accessible.

Soon Jim was running the show, overseeing all aspects of the business. At once affable and reserved, he guided the company onward and upward, constantly increasing production. Not content to rely on the success and popularity of just one brand, Beam branched out and tinkered with mash bills and recipes to produce new products, such as Clear Springs, Jefferson Club, and Pebbleford. This desire to innovate, to offer new whiskies with new tastes, was a trait his grandson would inherit.

These new brands, along with Old Tub, were highly regarded and Beam seemingly could do no wrong. As the Nelson County Register reported in 1896, "Mr. Beam does his own distilling and his product is not to be excelled by anyone." The paper went on to say that Jim was "full of energy . . . no one is more popular in this community than he." Thing were going well for Jim Beam, now known around town as Big B. The future looked promising.

With his wife Mary Catherine and three children—a son, T. Jeremiah, and two daughters, Margaret and Mimi—the Beams easily assumed their roles as prominent members of Kentucky society, hosting large parties at their formidable new home on North Third Street in Bardstown, which Beam had purchased in 1910. The home offered a wide front porch where he and good friends, including distiller T. W. Samuels, would often sit and discuss life and watch the buggies go by while sipping on something special. (The Samuels and Beams were close, literally and figuratively. They lived next door to each other.) The expression "he's as rich as Jim Beam" began popping up around town. Jim Beam took it as a compliment. He was king of the bourbon hill and there was nothing wrong with that.

Prohibition ended all of this. Forced to close up shop, Beam tried his hand at a series of unsuccessful ventures: citrus farming, coal mining, and finally the rock quarry out in Clermont. The quarry was located next door to the shuttered Murphy Barber distillery, which Beam had purchased during the first years of Prohibition with the hope that he would one day reopen it.

He waited 14 long years. When Prohibition was finally repealed on December 5, 1933, Beam, approaching 70, got the old distillery operational in just under three months. It took him close to a year to get financing, but when the loan was finally secured, the plant (renamed the James B. Beam Distillery) made its first official run of whiskey on March 25, 1935. The rebuilt distillery would soon be producing five brands, including Old Tub, F. G. Walker, Five Beams,

Cave Hollow, and Colonel James B. Beam (which in less than 10 years became simply Jim Beam Kentucky Straight Bourbon Whiskey).

Throughout this second act, Beam remained a hands-on boss, insistent on doing things a certain way. Above all, he was very protective of the family recipe, especially the yeast used to convert the starches in the mash into alcohol. Like all Beams, he was a practical distiller, which meant that the yeast he used came from a wild strain, as opposed to a strain cultivated in a laboratory. Yeast is critical in whiskey making. Each strain has a specific flavor that impacts the taste of the whiskey. According to Booker, his grandfather was obsessive about it. Every Friday, he carried home a jug of it in his car: if the distillery burned down over the weekend, he thought, at least the yeast would be safe.

Beam remained at the helm of the family business until 1944, promoting the company's brands around the country whenever he could. After selling the business to the Chicagoans, he enjoyed a short retirement, fishing and hunting. His favorite gun was a Winchester 12-gauge, which he gave to his 18-year-old grandson a week before Christmas. Booker, the excellent shot, went out and shot some quail, which he cleaned and cooked himself and then presented as a gift to his granddaddy. Jim and Booker ate the quail on Christmas Eve, and the very next day Jim died at the age of 83 in the same four-poster bed that Booker would one day occupy.

CHAPTER 2

College Ain't for Everyone

A fter Booker graduated from St. Joe's Prep, it was off to the University of Kentucky. Booker didn't really have much say in the matter. His college choice had been preordained by his uncle T. Jeremiah, Jim Beam's only son and the new patriarch of the family. T. Jeremiah—Uncle Jere—was a devoted UK alum who thought the sun rose and set over Lexington, so there had never been any doubt about where his star nephew was going. There was also never any doubt that Booker was going to play football there and join the Sigma Nu fraternity, the same house Jere had joined. He was going to be a Wildcat and that was that. Uncle Jere had it all figured out.

Booker had been a star at St. Joe's, earning All-State honors, leading sweeps on offense, and blowing up quarterbacks on defense. But playing at the next level for a Southeastern Conference team? Now that was entirely another matter. Especially an SEC team coached by an up-and-comer by the name of Paul "Bear" Bryant. While Booker liked playing football, he wasn't sure he was exactly Bear material.

Bryant apparently agreed. He offered Booker's best friend and cousin Bob Noe Hayden a scholarship but passed on the big kid from Bardstown.

"He's 50 pounds overweight," the Bear told a crestfallen Jere. "That boy's just too big."

Uncle Jere didn't take no for an answer, though, even from a man like Bryant. Personable and persuasive, and a loyal UK fundraiser, he talked the Bear into letting Booker walk on to the team, saying he'd be worth it.

"He'll get the weight down," he told Bryant. "You'll see."

"If he does, then he might be a player," the Bear said. "If he don't, he won't."

Booker had little to say about all of this. By all accounts, he was indifferent about playing for Kentucky. He wasn't sure what he wanted to do, but attending brutal two-a-day practices in the Kentucky heat, then sitting through hours of classes, wasn't necessarily high on his bucket list. Compounding matters was the fact that he had hurt his hand in a car accident over the summer and the injury had been slow to heal. His hand hurt like hell.

On top of everything else, there was Bob Gain to consider. Gain was a huge and strong All-American lineman (and eventual All-Pro NFL player). Bryant had Booker go head-to-head with him in practice, an assignment Booker did not relish.

"By God, Gain is killing me," he confided to a friend after a particularly brutal practice.

Still, he dutifully trudged out to the field with cousin Bob, a quick and agile cornerback. For two weeks he banged and bruised, his hand swelling up something fierce. At night he'd sit in his dorm room by an open window, feel the humid breeze on his face, and wonder why he was doing all of this. Partly it was because of Uncle Jere: he had great respect for the man. Partly it was because of his size: he was big, and big men, well, they played football. At least in Kentucky they did.

Bear apparently rode the boy about his weight, saying he had to drop some pounds fast if he was going to stick. Rather than being motivated, Booker stubbornly withdrew.

His father Pinkie found that out for himself one day in late August when he decided to surprise the boy at practice. He drove over to Lexington to see Booker in action and give him some encouragement, buck him up some. Strolling over to the field and squinting in the sun, he saw the Hayden boy running about, saw Bob Gain wreaking havoc, but no Booker. He watched and waited then finally asked an assistant coach, who informed him that Booker had quit the team.

"Well, I'll be damned," Pinkie said.

He strode purposefully across campus in search of Booker and found him sitting under a tree in the shade trying to feed peanuts to a squirrel.

"How come you're not at practice?" he asked.

"I'm done with practice, done with football."

"What the hell are you talking about?" Pinkie asked.

Booker tossed a peanut in the general direction of the squirrel. "I'm just done with playing," he said. "That's all."

"Then what the hell did you come to UK for?" Pinkie asked.

"That's the very question I've been asking myself," Booker said. "In fact, I'm starting to think that college ain't for everyone."

Booker ended up sticking around for the fall semester, and by all accounts he made the most of it. He and his buds had a big time in the dorm, carrying on with the coeds and enjoying maybe more than their share of the family elixir. Gregarious and likable, Booker had an affinity for good times, particularly dancing. The Big Man was Fred Astaire light on his feet, and the girls lined up for a chance to be twirled around the dance floor by Booker.

This went on until the beginning of the second semester. Then, without warning, Booker up and left Lexington.

"He just disappeared," said cousin Bob. "No one knew exactly where."

There were some reports that he was down South, others that he was still somewhere in Kentucky. His parents were worried. Their oldest son had vanished without a trace.

He finally surfaced weeks later in Albuquerque, New Mexico. He and his friend Billy had apparently been hitchhiking across the country, working odd jobs for food, and sleeping on the side of the road, if they slept at all. By the time they reached New Mexico they were tired and (as always) hungry. The vagabond life was not for them. So on a whim they decided to enlist in the Air Force. Three squares and a roof over their heads, maybe fly planes someday—plus, the Cold War was heating up and they would be serving their country.

As part of the routine background review, the Air Force recruiter called the sheriff in Springfield to check up on Booker. The sheriff gave Booker a good report, then called Pinkie and told him Booker had surfaced.

"Where is he?" Pinkie asked.

"New Mexico. About to join the Air Force."

"The Air what? Hell, can you picture that boy in the Air Force?"

The sheriff was quiet. "Don't suppose I can."

"He'd probably cause a war."

"Now that you mention it, that's a possibility, yes."

Pinkie got ahold of Booker and told him not to sign anything. Then he wired his son some money to come home. His friend Billy's family also wired him money, but rather than buying a bus ticket, Billy pocketed the cash. When Billy told Booker he was keeping the money and wasn't going home, Booker took umbrage.

"Hell, that's not right," he said. "Your folks, they gave you that money to go home."

"I ain't going. Money's mine now."

Booker thought on that for minute. Then he coldcocked Billy—laid him out flat.

"Damn you, Booker! What you do that for?" Billy yelled, rubbing his chin.

Booker hitched up his pants. "That's from your dad," he said.

Legend has it that Billy eventually enlisted in the Air Force anyway, where he had a long and successful career. Booker went back to Kentucky, though, where a very different future waited.

T. Jeremiah Beam

Booker's uncle, Thomas Jeremiah Beam, had a major influence on him. Personable and considered city slick, T. Jeremiah helped smooth out some of his nephew's rougher edges by teaching him salesmanship, promotion, and communication.

Born in 1899, T. Jeremiah, or Jere, was the oldest of three children. As the only son of Jim Beam, one of the country's most prominent distillers, there was little question that he would join the family business, which was thriving in the early 1900s. Like his father and his father's father and his father's father's father before him, he went to work at the distillery at a young age—13 years old—under the watchful eye of his family.

Jere learned everything he could about distilling and was considered fairly adept at the process by the time he was 20. But then Prohibition hit, and he was, as Booker would later say, "all dressed up with nowhere to go." So for a number of years he dutifully helped his father run a variety of businesses that were unrelated to making whiskey.

After Prohibition was repealed Jere took center stage, leading the reconstruction of the family distillery along with his 70-year-old father and his Uncle Park. He was so involved in the process that he moved onto the grounds and lived in a former boarding house with his wife, Lucy Kavanaugh. They lived there, in the shadow of the distillery, for a number of years.

Once the distillery was fully operational, Jim retired and left Jere to run the show with the investors who had bought the company. A natural salesman and communicator, Jere thrived in the leadership position, expanding Beam's markets to overseas cities, and increasing sales of the now-popular Jim Beam Bourbon by relentless promotion around the country. In 1953 he purchased a new distillery, called Plant Number Two, near Boston, Kentucky. As a result, production—and subsequently sales—continued to grow.

An avid sportsman, he loved college football and basketball and was a devoted alum of the University of Kentucky. Since he had no children, he grew close to his nephew Booker, whom he treated like a son. Early on he identified him as a possible heir to the family's bourbon throne. "Boy's got potential," he was reported to have said. "He just has to get focused."

Jere died in 1977. His likeness adorns the label on the famous Jim Beam Bourbon bottle, above his nephew's image.

CHAPTER 3

Fork in the Road

I n 1950, bourbon was in the midst of a furious comeback. With Prohibition, the Depression, and World War II safely in the rear view mirror, and quality, properly aged whiskey finally available, demand for the spirit increased at a rapid pace. People from coast to coast were rediscovering what their grandparents had known years before—this brown liquor from Kentucky, it's pretty darn good.

Cultural changes aided this growth. The fifties saw the advent of the cocktail hour, a nightly ritual that occurred after work in the confines of the suburban homes of America's burgeoning middle and upper classes. For decades, most alcohol consumption had taken place in bars, taverns, and speakeasies, but now it was socially acceptable to drink at home in the company of neighbors, friends, and family. Imbibing during the work day also became acceptable with the white-collar crowd, with deals being done and clients landed over two- and three-drink lunches. This growing affinity for all things alcohol included a desire for cocktails that featured bourbon, a highly mixable spirit. As a result, Manhattans and Old Fashioneds were in demand.

Another factor supporting the bourbon renaissance was the once-unattainable overseas market. During and immediately following World War II, Kentucky distilleries, especially Jim Beam, had shipped bourbon to American troops in Europe on U.S. Navy ships. The GIs were only too eager to share their whiskey with their hosts in Germany, France, the Netherlands, Belgium, and England. Consequently, Europeans fell in love and exports of bourbon soared to record highs. Seemingly overnight, the world had discovered bourbon—and it wanted more.

Booker didn't seem all that aware of the seismic changes that were taking place in the industry his family had helped to create. He returned to Springfield, his tail safely between his legs. With college apparently no longer an option, he took a job at a local lumberyard doing manual labor. Once again, he could outwork three men on a good day, hauling, loading, and cutting. His work ethic, his particular strength, became the stuff of legend. One day Bill Samuels Jr., the son of the distiller Bill Samuels of Maker's Mark fame, was driving home and saw two young women changing a tire on their Volkswagen Beetle at the side of the road. He slowed as he passed, then stopped completely when he came to the front of the car, not believing what he was seeing: there was Booker Noe, holding the end of the car up with his bare hands, as the girls scrambled underneath to finish the task.

"You need any help there, Booker?" Bill asked.

"Naw, I'm fine," Booker said.

"You sure?"

"Hell, it's just a damn Beetle. Pretty light."

After work, he hit the local establishments with aggressive delight. Springfield and the communities nearby offered a variety of drinking establishments, and Booker and his loyal posse were regulars, drinking beer with occasional shots of the family liquor, the bartenders obliging. Booker was the jovial center of things, swapping tales and jokes and playing cards. He only turned serious when the subject of his little brother Jerry came up.

Rumor had it that Jerry, who was in his early teens, had been making the rounds at local bars, looking to quench his thirst. If his brother could do it, so could he, he thought. Why should Booker have all the fun? Big Brother Booker, though, would have none of it.

"Don't you go serving him any alcohol," he warned bartenders. "He's not of age."

"Well, he comes by and he's asking for it."

"You tell him to go home and drink his milk. He's got to wait his turn."

After a few drinks, Booker and his boys would head over to a local dance club, the Jane Todd, and cut the rug; Booker showing his moves off in a way that impressed and delighted. On Saturdays there usually was a UK game to watch, and on Sundays there was fishing, hunting, and, of course, Margaret's fried chicken. Life was all good.

Over in Clermont life was pretty good, too. Uncle Jere, trying to make hay while the sun was shining, had ramped up production, adding workers and building rack houses in an attempt to meet the explosive demand for bourbon.

He had help. Carl, his cousin and Jim Beam's nephew, was now on the payroll. Still, more manpower was needed. And, as everyone in the industry knew, the best kind of manpower in the bourbon business was Beam manpower.

"What about hiring Booker on?" Uncle Jere asked Carl one morning. "We could use him."

Carl Beam, a reserved, no-nonsense man who enjoyed two things in life—working and working harder—was hesitant. As the newly appointed master distiller, the Clermont plant was his baby and he ran it with great keep-your-nose-to-the-grindstone, watch-every-dime efficiency. When it came to operating the distillery, suit-and-tie-wearing Uncle Jere had great respect for Carl and left him alone. Carl, he was The Man.

"Don't know about that, Jere," Carl said, wiping his hands with a rag.

"Why not? He's family."

"We got a lot of family down here. Every time you turn a corner in Kentucky, you bump into a damn Beam."

"Well, I'm just saying that maybe we should consider it, that's all."

"Boy's rambunctious."

"Well, maybe so. He's young and there's nothing wrong with being rambunctious at that age."

"This ain't the Jane Todd club, it's a distillery. No dancing."

"I understand that, Carl. But he's smart."

"Yeah, how'd UK work out? What, he's so smart, he gradu-ated in three months?"

"Okay, so he's maybe not book smart. But he's smart. As smart as anyone. You yourself know that to be true."

Carl squinted in the sunlight, down the hill toward the barreling room. A small group of men were standing outside of it, yapping and laughing, doing nothing. This annoyed Carl. He wasn't paying anyone to yap and laugh. He'd have a quiet talk with them when their shift ended.

"Think about it is all I'm saying."

"Don't know about that, Jere," Carl said, heading down the hill. "Don't know about that at all."

Uncle Jere dropped the subject temporarily, but down deep he wanted his nephew in the business and he kept after Carl, broaching the subject whenever he could. But Carl remained unconvinced and uncommitted. Running a distillery was a huge responsibility. He didn't have time to keep an eye on his fun-loving young cousin who was already close to achieving hall of fame status in Kentucky bars and taverns. Besides, Carl wasn't the only one who had reservations. Others at the distillery shared his view. Booker, he was a live wire. Too hot to touch.

Things changed one day when Booker, who was still working at the lumberyard, got a phone call from Thompson Willett, a local distiller. Thompson, it seemed, wanted Booker to come work with him at Willett in Bardstown.

"You offering me a job?" Booker asked.

"Yes I am. You can start Monday."

"I don't know anything about distilling," Booker said.

"You're a Beam. You know more than you think. We'll teach you the rest. Besides, you want to spend the rest of your life in a lumberyard?"

Booker fell quiet. "Let me think on it."

"Take your time. We'd love to have you."

Booker mulled over this opportunity for a few days. Willett was a reputable place producing a number of quality whiskies, such as the fine-tasting Old Bardstown. He bounced the idea off his friends, who told him to take it: it would be more interesting than the lumberyard, plus the pay was better.

"A real opportunity," they said. "And you probably can get us free whiskey."

Still Booker mulled. Something about working at Willett didn't sit just right. Finally, he told his mother about the job. He had great respect for his mother; she was one of the few people who could put and keep him in his place, and he wanted her opinion.

After listening to her son, Margaret thought that this was a step in the right direction. Her father, Jim, had thought Booker had potential and more than once had mentioned that he could make a living working at a distillery one day. Unfortunately, Willett probably wasn't the distillery he had in mind.

"You want to go work there?" she asked.

"Thinking about it. Beats the lumberyard, I guess."

"That's not much of a reason to pick a career. Do you want to make bourbon?"

"I could. But I don't know much about it."

"You can learn. It's a fine business and it's time you start thinking long term about your life. No one's going to pay you for drinking and dancing. You've come to the fork in the road, Booker. Time to make the right choice. This is a solid livelihood. Been good to our family for years. Might be time to get into it."

Booker, of course, was starting to think the same thing. Up until this point in his life, distilling and whiskey making hadn't had much of a hold on him. His father wasn't in the business and many of his dozens of cousins weren't either. Despite his blood line, there had been little pressure to go in that direction. While bourbon had been a constant in his life, something that was always there, he had never given much thought about making it. He was proud of being a Beam, of course, but he didn't feel an obligation to follow in his ancestors' footsteps. Truth be told, he had never given the subject much thought one way or another.

Still, the times he had visited the distillery he had liked what he saw. The work had interested him. The gurgling yeast vats, the column still, the barrels stacked together in an orderly way. Everything with a purpose, everything with a place. From his perspective it was a respectable trade, and one he might like. Also, he had loved his granddaddy and respected the hell out of him. If his granddaddy had done it, then maybe he should too.

"Booker, are you there?"

"I'm here."

"So, are you interested?

"I suppose I am."

"Good. And you're not going to work at Willett, I can tell you that right now. I know it's a good place, but you're going to work for your uncle over at Beam. Your grandfather's company. What do you think he would say if you went somewhere else? How do you think he'd feel?"

"He wouldn't be pleased, I guess."

"That's an understatement. If you want, I can call your uncle."

"Naw, don't do that. Put him on the spot. They don't have a job for me anyway."

"They'll make room for you. Now go on and call him. Tell him that you're interested, tell him about Willett too."

"Maybe I will."

When Margaret hung up she was unconvinced that her son would make the call. She suspected that he was embarrassed over what had happened at UK and that he didn't want to ask Jere for a favor. She picked up the phone herself.

"Willett?" Jere said. "Well, I'll be damned."

"If my son's going to work at a distillery, by God it's going to be the Jim Beam distillery," Margaret said. "You hire him on, Jere."

Jere chewed on his lip. "I hear you, Margaret," he said. "I hear you."

"Call him today."

"Slow down now, slow down. It's not that easy. In fact, it's a little complicated. First of all, we don't really have a job for him."

"What's so complicated? You want him working for a competitor? How's that going to look? Our father would roll over in his grave."

Jere chewed on his lip harder. "That might be so," he said. "But there's lots of Beams working at different plants. There's pretty much a Beam at every distillery in Kentucky, you know that. There's Park over at Heaven Hill, then there's cousin Elmo . . ."

"This is Booker, Jere. Booker. Jim Beam's grandson. His *grandson*."

Jere let out a sigh. "I know who Booker is. Believe me, I know who he is," he softly said. Then he said he'd see what he could do.

Jere thought on things for a while, did his own mulling. On one hand, he understood the hesitancy about hiring Booker. To be sure, he was a handful. Plus, there was what had happened at UK to consider. Booker up and quit on him, Uncle Jere thought—after all the strings I pulled to get him on that damn team, he up and quit. Then he did his vanishing act, hitchhiking and hoboing across the country, doing who knows what. What happens if I bring him on, and he pulls a similar stunt? Here today, gone tomorrow? By God, we'd be the laughing stock of the entire industry. Carl had some very valid concerns. Very valid. Booker Noe was as unpredictable as spring weather and hiring him was a risky proposition.

But he was a hard worker, Jere had seen that with his own eyes. The boy was strong as an ox. He was also smart and had the gift of gab.

Plus, Booker was blood: no small thing. *A Beam.* A direct descendant of Jim and David M. and David and Jacob. The next in line. He had even lived in the Beam house for a year after Jim died. *A Beam.*

Last, but certainly not least, Booker was his boy. Jere didn't have any children, and despite Booker's shortcomings—the dancing, the drinking, the UK thing—Jere still thought the world of him. It was impossible not to like that boy, impossible. In the end, Uncle Jere decided that the rewards outweighed the risks. He'd roll the dice and offer his nephew a job.

He had to finesse things, though, proceed carefully, use his diplomatic skills. He didn't want to play boss on Carl, he had too much respect for the man. Hardworking and honest, Carl was the backbone of the company. No sir, he didn't want to play boss. There had to be another way.

Sitting alone in his office, he considered options, and then he came up with a plan. Yes, sir, this might just work—yes, sir, this had a chance. He picked up the phone and called Mr. Harry Blum of Chicago, the owner of the company.

"Harry? Hello there, this here is Jere. I'm fine, I'm fine, thanks for asking. Listen, I was wondering if I could ask you a favor now. It's a little complicated, so hear me out. It's about my nephew Booker. Yes, that's right, that's right. Yes, that's his real name. Booker."

CHAPTER

4

Starting Out

Booker started his career working for the Jim Beam Distilling Company at the Clermont plant on September 5, 1951. He showed up on time, his lunch packed, shiny new, laced-up work boots on and ready to go. Cousin Carl showed him around and gave him the overview of the place. While Booker had been there before, this time he took things in with keen eyes. He had a vague understanding of what everything was and what it did, but he needed to know more—lots more. So he made an effort to pay attention and listen to Carl's every word, even though some of the things Carl was saying were fairly basic.

They were standing by the railroad tracks near the front of the distillery. "Over here is where we unload the grain from the trains and take it to get mashed up," Carl said. He glanced at his watch and started to walk fast. He really didn't have time for this—the suits from Chicago were coming down today for a meeting that Jere wanted him at, and one of the fermenting tanks had to be checked because it might have a leak—but still he pressed on, showing Booker the ropes as best he could.

"We take the grain, the corn and rye, and the malted barley and grind it all up, make it look like meal, then add some water and cook it all together over there," he said pointing to a building in the distance. "We don't have time to go there now. You can go there on your own."

"I've been there," said Booker.

"Go again."

"Okay, I will."

"Now once we get the mash cooked up, do you know what we do next?"

Booker wasn't sure. He really didn't know as much about distilling as people might have thought he did. Most of his knowledge of the family business was on the consumption end. "You add the yeast?" he asked.

"That's right. We add the yeast. The family yeast. Your granddaddy was a distiller and a yeast maker. This yeast, it's been around since the thirties. Your granddaddy Jim, he made it. We keep a close eye on it. When we close down for the summer, I take about 15 gallons of it to Merchants Ice and Cold Storage in Louisville for safekeeping. We don't take no chances. Don't want to have to make another yeast. This is the best one. Don't mess with it."

"Why would I mess with it?"

Carl shot Booker a look. "I won't mess with it," Booker said.

They crossed the grounds and entered a building. It was hot and humid inside and smelled sweet. Together they climbed stairs, Booker huffing and puffing while Carl took two at a time. They finally stopped in front of a huge cypress tank. Booker suddenly remembered this place in a flashback. His granddaddy had brought him here for the first time when he was 10 years old. He recalled standing over these tanks and sniffing the grains, watching the mash move like it was alive as it rolled from side to side, belching gas. Booker had worried that the mash was going to roll over the sides and spill out.

"Okay," Carl continued. "Here's where we put the mash— the grain mixture—and then we add the yeast. What does the yeast do now?"

"It turns the mash into alcohol."

"That's right, more or less."

Booker surprised himself by knowing that. "My granddaddy told me that."

"He did?"

"A long time ago."

"Well, these here are fermenters." Carl motioned for Booker to step close to the tank. "Put your head in there now, take a deep breath. Go on now."

Booker did as he was told, and when he inhaled, his head kicked back so hard, he worried that he'd hurt his neck. The smell of the fermenting liquid was overpowering. "Damn," he said. "Strong stuff."

"Sure is. We let it ferment for about three or four days. We call it distiller's beer. Stick your finger in there and taste it. Go on, go on."

Booker had done this before, but he did it again.

"Go on now, taste it."

Booker licked a finger and tasted oatmeal. "Tastes pretty good," he said.

"It will taste better once we distill it. Come on."

They crossed over the wooden floor, out a side door, and made their way down some steps toward the actual distillery. The room was a mass of pipes and pumps, and it was noisy. In the center of the room was a tall column made of steel that shot straight up.

"You know what happens here?" Carl asked.

Booker started to say yes, but decided instead to shrug.

Carl spoke loudly, over the din of the place. "This is where we take the liquid—the distiller's beer—and turn it into high-proof alcohol. It's already beer when it gets to this point. We run it through this still, this column, heat it up and turn the alcohol into vapor. Then we cool that vapor and bring it back down to liquid form. That liquid has a lot more alcohol in it. We call that liquid low wine. We then take that low wine and do it again, run it through the doubler over there." Carl pointed to another still, this one squat. It looked like a large pot. "When we cool it back down, it becomes liquid again. We call that high wine or white dog. Higher proof whiskey. You getting all this?"

Booker slowly nodded. This whole process was more complicated than he'd thought. Carl was throwing *a lot* of information at him. "Why's it called white dog?"

"Look at it, it's white. Clear. And if you drink too much of that, it will bite you on the ass like a dog."

Again Booker nodded. He would have to learn to respect white dog. He didn't want his ass bitten if he could avoid it.

"Guess I'll keep that dog on a leash," he said.

Carl smiled. "Come on, now."

Booker followed Carl back outside and they quickly crossed the grounds, walking up a gradual hill. Carl's house was at the top of the hill and his wife, Edna, was standing on the porch shaking out a short rug.

Booker gave Edna a wave and wondered what she was making for lunch. She was a good cook. Edna waved back.

"Come on, over here, come on," Carl said as they veered off to the right.

"Going to the rack house?"

"Yes. Poke our heads in and then I got to go."

On the periphery of the distillery stood the mighty Beam rack houses: large, silent sentinels made of corrugated tin and wood. Black fungus grew on the sides of the buildings, giving them a worn and mysterious look. Booker always liked the rack houses. His grandfather had taken him here once or twice when he was a boy and he had been in awe of them. Dark and peaceful, this is where his family's whiskey grew up, Granddaddy Jim said.

They stepped inside the dark building, and Booker took a deep breath. Cool, sweet air filled his lungs. This was a special place.

"We got about 200,000 barrels aging on the property," Carl said. "Dirt floors, no heat. We take a cross-section of barrels from different floors and dump the liquid out, marrying it all together. We do that over there, in the dump room. I'll show you that later."

Booker took a step further into the rack house, looked up, and saw hundreds of barrels stacked overhead. "How long do they stay here?"

"By law the whiskey has to stay in those barrels for at least two years, but we keep it longer, about four years. We have some liquid that's older. Like I said, we marry them all together in the dump room."

"What are the barrels made of?"

"White oak. We get them burned, have them charred on the inside, get a nice charcoal layer going."

"We do that here?"

"Naw, barrel maker does that. Once we get the barrels charred though, we put the new whiskey into them. It goes in white and pure. The white dog. Looks like water. When it comes out it looks like bourbon, reddish brown. See, the wood gives it color and some taste. Those barrels are important. Can't make bourbon without them. We can only use them once."

"Who says that?"

"The law says that and we better abide by it. If we reuse barrels we can't call it bourbon."

"Why oak?"

"Oak is porous but sturdy. The grain of the wood is good at holding the liquid in the barrel, but it's porous enough so the whiskey can flow in and out, back and forth. During the winter it gets cold in here, and whiskey, see, it contracts. In the summer, the whiskey expands and seeps into the barrel. Ebb and flow, that's what we're talking about here. These barrels go in full, but we lose 4 percent a year due to evaporation."

This fact startled Booker. "You mean, the whiskey evaporates?"

"Damn right it does. You know what we call that evaporation? The angels' share."

"The angels' share," Booker repeated. "Now that you say it, it rings a bell. Heard about that."

"Part of the business. Nothing we can do about it."

"Can't we make better barrels? Four percent seems like an awful waste."

"Hell, those angels got a right to drink. Keeps them on friendly terms with us. When we get to the pearly gates, maybe we can call in a few favors."

"Keeping angels happy can't hurt, I guess." Booker stared a long time at the barrels, his interest level high. Carl knew that Booker wasn't easily impressed, but he could tell he was impressed now. He glanced again at his watch. "Come on over here, come on, hurry up now."

Carl led Booker across the rack-house floor. As they walked, Booker noticed a number of batteries on the ground. He even stepped on one.

"What are these batteries for?" he asked.

Carl shook his head with some disgust, leaned down, and picked one up. "Leak hunters. We got men who crawl around all day looking for leaks in the barrels. If they find one, they got to plug it on up. They have flashlights and they leave the batteries lying around all over the damn place. I keep talking to them about it, but they keep leaving them. Make a mess."

"Will I be doing that?"

"Leak hunting?" Carl shook his head again, but this time he laughed. "Hell, I don't think you'd fit under many barrels, do you? Come on now."

They ended up on the far side of the rack house and finally stopped in front of a barrel.

"See this barrel?" Carl said. "What's different about it?"

Booker studied the barrel. Unlike the others in the rack house, it looked like it had been polished.

"It's clean," Booker said. "Someone cleaned it."

"It's shiny, is what it is. You know why it's shiny? Because some of our fellas rest their bellies on it while they're sneaking a drink. Their guts knock the dust off it. They don't think I know what they're doing, but I do. I know everything that goes on here, everything. I *live* here. This must be a good barrel because it's so damn shiny. Here." Carl took a wooden mallet and banged on each side of the barrel, popping the cork, or bung, out. He then reached behind the barrel and produced a short copper tube and stuck it in the barrel and drew some whiskey out.

"What's that?"

"Called a thief. We use it to get the whiskey. Look around for a cup," he told Booker. "This barrel's so shiny there's probably a dozen of them laying around. Probably some mules too."

"Mules?"

"Tell you about that later. Hurry up now, come on."

Booker searched around on the ground and sure enough he found a cup and held it out. Carl released the whiskey from the tube and it flowed right into it.

"Take a sip now."

Booker obliged. Warm whiskey filled his mouth, slightly sweet. He closed his eyes and thought he tasted hints of caramel and vanilla. He then swallowed and felt his body grow warm. He had drunk his share of whiskey, obviously, but nothing like this.

"Damn," he said.

"Damn right," Carl said, banging the bung back into place. "That's what we're selling."

Booker took another sip. While the first drink was good, the second one was better.

"That's enough, now," Carl said, taking the cup away. "All right, you'll start in the distillery. That's where you're going to be spending some time. You'll be working at everything here, getting experience and learning the ropes from the others, but mostly you're going to be learning the distilling side of the business. That's the heart of things. I'll teach you what I can, but I don't have that much time. So you're going to have to keep your eyes and ears open and take in everything. Know when to help, and know when to stay out of the way. You won't learn it all in one day. I've been here for more than 20 years, and I'm still learning."

"All right," Booker said.

"Just ask questions, and if I got time, I'll answer them."

"Okay, I will. Thanks for the chance."

Carl looked hard at his cousin, a big man, with a friendly face, and eyes that took things in. Knew when to talk, knew when to listen. Inside Carl's top desk drawer in his office was a letter from Mr. Harry Blum in Chicago asking him, in so many words, to hire Booker. When Carl got the letter, he knew what he had to do and he did it, no more questions asked. He wasn't sure where all this was heading, but at least for today, he was glad he had hired Booker on. Maybe Jere was right. Booker, he had some potential.

"All right then," Carl said. "Let's go to it."

Letter from Harry Blum

July 27, 1951
Office of the Chairman of the Board

Dear Carl:
I am happy to know Jere has been talking to you about his nephew and am sure you and Jere will try to develop this boy and teach him the distilling business in the old traditional way, because some day you, Jere, and I will be in a different world and we need some young folks to carry on. I know Jere has been reluctant to talk to you about this. Hiring the boy isn't a must, but I think it is a good idea.

Kind regards to you and your family, and I hope I can get down to the plant soon and say hello to all the boys.

Sincerely,
Harry Blum

How Bourbon Is Made

There are five steps involved in the making of bourbon. Each one plays a vital role.

1. **Cooking.** Milled corn is mixed with pure limestone water and cooked at a very high temperature. The temperature is lowered and ground-up rye is added.

2. **Mashing.** After the grain mixture has cooked, the temperature is lowered again and the barley malt is added. This begins the mashing process. At this stage, an enzyme is released from the barley malt that converts grain starch into sugars. When conversion is complete, the mash is transferred to fermenters.

3. **Fermentation.** Yeast is added to the mash to begin the fermentation process. Yeast is a microorganism that converts sugar into alcohol. Each strain of yeast imparts a distinctive flavor and aroma to the finished whiskey and each distiller has a preferred strain. Distillers have spent years perfecting their own strains of yeast. The various strains used for Booker's and other Beam bourbons have been passed down in the Beam family for years.

4. **Distillation.** When fermentation is complete, mash, now called *distiller's beer*, is pumped into the still. The still is a 60-foot-tall column with a copper-sieve plate that runs across it. Inside the column, mash entering from the top meets steam rising from the bottom. The steam vaporizes the alcohol in the mash and carries it out from the top of the column into pipes, where it cools and condenses back into a liquid. The product of the first distillation is called *low wine*. This liquid is then distilled again in the *doubler*, a smaller still shaped like a pot. The doubler is sometimes referred to as the *thumper*, since it can make a thumping sound while distilling. The product of the second distillation

(*continued*)

(continued)

is called *high wine* or *white dog*. It can also be referred to as *green whiskey*.

5. **Aging.** White dog is as clear as water. Bourbon's distinctive color—and much of its flavor—comes from its aging time in wood. The longer bourbon is aged, the more flavor it takes from the wood. By law, bourbon must be aged in new charred oak barrels for at least two years. Charring caramelizes sugars in the wood, which slowly dissolve into the resting whiskey.

5

The Student

Booker spent the next two years at the Clermont plant learning the ropes. He worked in the dump room, the rack houses, the fill room, and in the distillery, doing some of this and some of that. For the most part he kept his head low and his eyes open. He worked hard and took things in. He asked a lot of questions and then asked more. Carl was a good source of information, of course, as were the other workers. There was general speculation that Booker was being groomed for big things, so his inquisitiveness was encouraged.

Every so often Uncle Jere would check in to see how he was doing. He'd jump out of his Cadillac and slap Booker on the back. While the whole family seemed to be keeping an eye on him, Uncle Jere was the most interested in his progress.

"How's it going there, Booker?" Uncle Jere would ask.

"All right."

"You picking all this up?"

"Much as I can."

"What interests you the most?"

"The distilling end, I guess."

"That's what I figured. Keep at it."

"I aim to."

After work, Booker still had energy to party. He was in his early twenties and had some oats to sow. He had a tight-knit group of friends—some from St. Joe's, others from Bardstown and Springfield—a loyal bunch who would stay with him for life. Together they hit the honky-tonks until the wee hours, enjoying each other's company as well as the companionship of the local girls. Having an inner circle of friends, an entourage, was important to Booker. He was comfortable with a crowd around him: he needed and wanted companionship. The more the merrier. As far as Booker was concerned, life wasn't worth living if you were living it alone. So it was off to the Jane Todd, or the Fish and Game Club, or the Lincoln Tavern over in New Haven, to have a few and maybe cut the rug some, Booker jitterbugging like nobody's business. "My girlie dancing," he would call it.

There was a price to pay for this revelry, though: mornings at the distillery could come pretty damn early.

"You got the flu or something?" Uncle Jere would ask.

"Naw, just moving a little slow, that's all."

"You move any slower, you'd be a tree. You know, Booker, we're not making all this whiskey for you and your boys to drink. We got other customers too. Make sure you leave some for them."

"We'll do our best."

"Someone told me they saw you with that Wickham girl."

"Yeah, we went out. Went dancing the other day."

"She's a nice girl."

They were talking about Annis Wickham, a young Bardstown gal. They had met in Dr. Wheat's (the dentist's) office. Booker was sitting in the chair, his mouth already open and waiting to have his teeth cleaned, when in walked this young hygienist, Annis, as pretty a little thing as there ever was. Booker took one look at her and opened his mouth even wider. Hellfire, he thought, I've got to go to the damn dentist more often. They went on their first date two weeks later, after a mutual friend made formal introductions.

"She's a nice girl," Uncle Jere said again. "Quiet and steady. Her type would keep a man grounded, focused."

"I suppose so."

"Could make a man a fine wife."

"Imagine she could."

Uncle Jere winked at Booker, then gave his back one more slap. "All right then."

"All right then."

Despite his social life, Booker showed up to work every day on time and put in a full day. He was a jack-of-all-trades, fixing this, overseeing that. The other workers, some of whom had initially been suspicious (if not downright resentful) of Booker, the boss's nephew, warmed to him. He wasn't a spy and he wasn't playing boss. Despite holding the title of supervisor, he was one of them, another working Kentucky boy making a living by making bourbon.

And a lot was being made. Bourbon's growth was continuing and Uncle Jere was ramping up production, adding workers and equipment to keep the whiskey flowing. Sometime in early 1953, though, he came to the realization that adding shifts and employees wasn't enough. He had to increase production in a different, more sustainable way.

In October of 1953, the company leased the shuttered Churchill Distillery near Boston, Kentucky from a local competitor. This plant, which for decades would simply be known as Plant Number Two, had good access to water and three usable rack houses. Otherwise the distillery was a mess, so Uncle Jere called on the one man he knew who could get it operational: Carl Beam. Hard-working Cousin Carl went at it, a man with a mission. With help from his son Baker, as well as from Booker, he built new fermenters and repaired the boiler. What he couldn't fix, he bought, and what he bought, he bought cheap. Why buy a new electric motor to agitate the mash when he could get one used? There were plenty of old but perfectly good distillery parts lying around Kentucky, and Carl found them. In addition to being hard working, Carl was also frugal; the man watched every dime, a trait that Jere admired. Under Carl's supervision, the distillery was gradually resurrected.

In 1954 the Boston plant officially opened for business. There was no fanfare. No cake or ribbon cutting to mark the occasion, no announcements in the press, no speeches about the future from one of the Chicago suits. This was a make-up plant, and its original goal was simple: distill what Clermont couldn't handle. Plant Number Two, that's all this was. Back-up quarterback. When the bosses from Chicago came down, they weren't coming here. No, sir. Neither would any visitors or tourists. This was in-country, a whiskey outpost plain and simple. Plant Number Two.

Once he got it going, Carl decided to head back to the hustle and bustle of Clermont. He had been splitting his days between the two plants and couldn't keep it up. Production was growing in the Clermont distillery and it needed more of his time and attention. Besides, the Clermont plant was home, literally. It was where he lived.

"Who you going to put in charge?" Uncle Jere asked. "Baker?"

"Hell no, he's too young. I need him out in Clermont anyway."

"Who then? Thinking of hiring? I can ask around."

"I'm thinking it will be Booker."

"Booker? You mean *our* Booker?"

"You know anyone else named Booker?"

"Hell, you think he's ready?"

"We'll find out," Carl said.

Carl Beam

Carl Beam, son of Park Beam and nephew of Jim Beam, was born in 1908. As a youth he spent his days working on the family farm in Nelson County, then he headed off to college in Bowling Green. Money was tight, though, and in 1932 Carl was forced to drop out. He moved to California to work for the Civilian Conservation Corps, a public relief program for unemployed, unmarried men. It was part of Roosevelt's New Deal. Carl stayed in

(continued)

(continued)

California until Jim Beam called him back to Kentucky to work at his recently purchased rock quarry and later at the family distillery, which he helped to restore after Prohibition. When the plant opened for business, he was appointed first a distiller, then master distiller, then vice president in charge of the Clermont and Boston plants. During his tenure, Jim Beam Bourbon would become the leading bourbon in America.

As master distiller he was mentor, role model, and boss to his two sons, Baker and David (both of whom would rise to become distillers themselves), and his cousin Booker Noe (who would later hold the title of master distiller at Jim Beam). While his relationship with his cousin was at times strained and contentious, they both had a tremendous amount of respect for each other and shared a common commitment to their family and their bourbon.

Hard working, unpretentious, and gifted at producing whiskey, Carl is regarded as the unsung hero of the Beam dynasty, a vital link in the long generational chain. Carl's low-key nature kept him from the limelight and he was more comfortable behind the scenes. Reportedly turning down opportunities to become a spokesperson and the face of the company, he instead focused on the continued production of his family's whiskey. He was so closely linked to the distillery that he lived on its grounds for 28 years.

Carl retired from Beam in 1974 and died in 1981.

CHAPTER

6

Sweet Home Boston

At the ripe old age of 25, Booker Noe was placed in charge of Plant Number Two in Boston. He was given full responsibility for the place: He was distiller, human resource director, and warehouse supervisor. If it happened in Boston, Booker was now responsible for it. Despite being over in Clermont, Carl checked on him plenty. He was Booker's boss, make no mistake about that. Business was booming and things had to run right at both plants if production was going to be maintained.

One of Booker's first tasks was to do some hiring. While a handful of workers from Clermont had been transferred over to the plant, other spots needed to be filled, so Booker busied himself with finding the right people for those jobs. He scoured the area looking for men with distillery experience, asking for recommendations from other plants. When he heard of some-one with potential, he called him up and told him to come down for an interview. These so-called interviews were usually wide-open discussions that lasted either minutes or hours, depending on Booker's mood and interest level. One worker was hired after just five minutes: "You seem like an okay feller. But if you ever lie to me, you're fired." Another sat through a two-hour discourse on hunting and fishing, complete with Booker demonstrating the best way to cast a line into a creek.

In addition to men with experience, Booker also hired friends—men whose only qualification was that he liked them. The men he chose were appreciative: Beam was a good place to work, and they were eager to show their appre-ciation by putting forth a good effort at the plant. In addition to wanting to earn their pay, they wanted to show Booker that he had made the right choice by taking a chance on them.

Eventually Booker assembled a team he was comfortable with; a group of men he trusted. Once again he had his entourage, an inner circle that he could shoot the breeze with, work with, drink with, and, on occasion, fight with. This diverse bunch of men had one thing in common: They were all loyal to one Mr. Booker Noe.

While there had been some concerns about Booker's matu-rity and his ability to handle his new responsibilities, he put them to rest early in his tenure in Boston. While he was still a fun-loving man at night and on the weekends, he took his job seriously. No detail was too small, no task too hard. He poured his heart and soul into the distillery, learning as he went. After some hesitation, he now embraced his heritage and accepted the family legacy. Making bourbon was what he was supposed to do, what he was meant to do. He realized that now with fierce clarity.

"So Booker, he's doing all right?" Uncle Jere would ask Carl.

"I check up on him regular. He's keeping busy that's for sure. Boy won't stop. He's into everything over there."

"Busy is good," Uncle Jere said. "I like busy."

The old plant kept Booker more than busy. It was in need of constant maintenance, constant repair. Something, it seemed, was always breaking down and a breakdown could lead to a shutdown and a shutdown would lead to lost production. So shutting down was not an option.

The whiskey had to keep flowing. The demand was there. The American bourbon boom was in full swing in the mid to late fifties. As suburbia continued to grow, and with happy hours and cocktail parties now a permanent fixture in American culture, more and more people wanted a spirit that could be mixed or stand on its own. Bourbon was that spirit. Whether it was a Manhattan, an Old Fashioned, or a bourbon with a splash of water, people were enjoying it like never before.

The numbers bear this out: In 1945, bourbon accounted for less than 10 percent of bottled whiskey. By 1950, that number had grown to 25 percent. And in 1961, bourbon accounted for exactly half of all bottled whiskey sales in America.

As Booker threw himself into his work, Annis (now his girlfriend) noticed a change in him. The happy-go-lucky guy she had fallen for was growing into a responsible, work-obsessed man. While the change was for the good (she knew that), she was seeing less and less of her man. It didn't take her long to realize that Booker had a new love in his life, a mistress she couldn't compete against.

"You're spending too much time over there," she would say.

"I got a lot to do."

"Sometimes I think you love that plant more than you love me."

Booker thought about that. "I admit, I'd sleep in the rack house if they let me."

"You should just go marry that old distillery."

"I asked, but the priest won't allow it."

Booker married Annis instead. Their wedding on April 7, 1956, was attended by a who's who of Bardstown. They drove down to New Orleans for their honeymoon, had dinner at Pat O'Brien's, and got themselves an apartment in Bardstown when they returned, just a few blocks from the Big House on North Third Street. A job, a wife, a home: all that Booker needed now was a son to complete the picture, and soon he had one. On March 9, 1957, Frederick Booker Noe III was born. Booker drove his newborn home from the hospital in Louisville in a brand new Fairlane and showed him off to friends and family.

"Another generation," he said, holding his son up high for everyone to see.

"One more Beam," Uncle Jere said, passing around a bottle.

"Yes sir, but this one's special because this one's mine," Booker said.

Baby Fred was just the latest in the large and seemingly ever-growing brood of Beams in Kentucky. While there was no official count, the number of descendants of Jacob Beam in the Commonwealth listed in the hundreds. (Jacob had started the ball rolling by having 12 children himself.) Consequently, the family was huge. And an inordinate number of them went into the distilling business, the vast majority working for

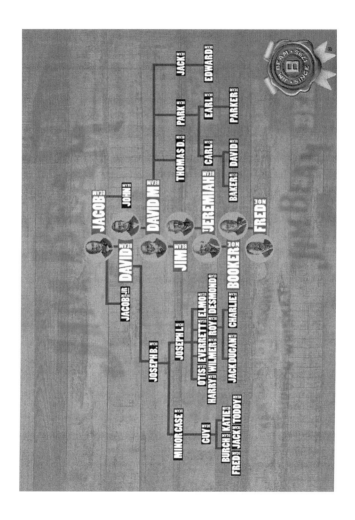

whiskey makers *other* than Jim Beam. There was Earl Beam over at Heaven Hill, and Elmo at Maker's Mark, and then, of course, Jack, Jim Beam's uncle and best man at his wedding, who had started up Early Times. There was also (in no particular order and to just name a few) Otis, Minor, Roy, Joe, Everett, and Harry; all of them cousins and all of them distillers. The expression "Behind every bourbon is a Beam" wasn't just catchy—it was true.

Booker, and now his son, Fred, had the distinction of being direct descendants of the most famous Beam of all, however: Jim Beam. It was a distinction that Booker was aware of and very proud of. But, as he knew, a name and family can only get you so far. Eventually you have to prove yourself, stand on your own two feet. Working at Plant Number Two, Booker listened and learned as much as he could, and waited to make his own mark.

CHAPTER 7

Proving Himself

A comfortable and predictable routine took hold of Booker's life as he entered his thirties. He moved his family next door to the Big House in Bardstown to be closer to Aunt Mimi, Jim Beam's daughter. Annis got a job as a medical technician at the local hospital and little Freddie grew fast. The family received bad news in 1963, when Booker's father, Pinkie, died of a heart attack while walking across Stoll Field in Lexington after a UK game. "I think I need to sit down," he said, clutching at his chest, and just like that he was gone, passing away on sacred ground.

Despite this unexpected setback, Booker's career continued its upward trek. He logged long hours at the distillery, frequently arriving at the plant before seven. After putting his lunch (usually a meat sandwich of some kind) on the top of a steam pipe to keep it warm, he would make a slow and thorough inspection of things. Booker liked things just so.

"Big Man's here," the workers would yell when they saw him coming.

"Damn right I'm here," Booker would yell back. "Damn right."

His first stop was the rack houses, where he would check in with his brother-in-law Jimmy Wickham. Since Jimmy was family Booker would make it a point to be tough on him, because he never wanted to be accused of playing favorites. After quizzing Jimmy on the state of the aging barrels and after he received what he thought were acceptable answers, he'd head down to one of the two lakes on the property to gauge their levels. Water is what makes a distillery run, so Booker kept a keen eye on the lakes. If the levels got too low they would pump more water in from nearby Wilson Creek.

While surveying the water he might run into the government man, the federal employee who was stationed at the Boston plant. The man literally held the keys to the plant, unlocking it in the morning so workers could enter. For years government men, called gaugers, oversaw whiskey-producing plants, making sure that the bourbon that was aging wasn't sold before its time and that each barrel was accounted for and taxed appropriately. Booker never had any issues with any of the government men he worked with. Hell, they were just doing their jobs and he had nothing to hide.

After a friendly chat with the man he'd head over to the distillery, where he'd confer with the plant chemist. There he'd check on the pH level and the ballings, or sugar content, of the mash to make sure both were in line. He would then take a walk over to the fermenting tanks to make sure they too were operational. Then it was off to the granary, where he would bite into a kernel of corn to test its moisture level. The corn was important because it made up most of the mash bill; if it was too dry or too wet, Booker would send it back. If he was satisfied that everything was fine, he'd finally (and somewhat reluctantly) head to his office, a small room with cinder-block walls by the grain-loading area. Booker wasn't much into paperwork and there usually was a stack of it waiting for him. With a heavy sigh, he would sit and wade through it, shuffling paper from one pile to the next. Carl would call some mornings to ask questions about this or that, but for the most part he now left Booker alone. Plant Number Two was his to run. He'd been thrown into the deep end of the pool years before, and for the most part he'd taught himself to swim. Carl now respected him for that. His younger cousin had done all right; he'd grown into the position and become a man. Uncle Jere too was pleased. His gamble had paid off. Booker was now a full-fledged distiller.

"All the reports are that you're doing pretty good," he'd say.

"Doing all right."

"You're putting out almost as much whiskey as Clermont."

"When the place is working right, no reason not to," Booker would say.

"Well, you're doing all right."

Pleasing Uncle Jere was a motivating factor in Booker's life. He regretted what had happened at the University of Kentucky, and had made up his mind to set things right. He knew his uncle had taken a chance on hiring him at the distillery and failing again was simply not an option. Every day he felt he needed to prove himself, so he did what needed to be done and then some.

Overall, he didn't care much what people thought of him. But with his uncle it was a different story. He wanted Jere to be proud of him.

Booker made his share of mistakes, of course. He once let some of the precious Beam family yeast sour when he forgot to power up the refrigerator one night. Yeast has to be kept cool, something Carl reminded him of loudly the next day. He had also experimented with mixing sawdust with the coal, thinking it would be an extra source of fuel. It didn't work, and after a number of attempts Booker ceased trying. These miscues aside, Booker had things on solid ground in Boston. Production was accelerating, and the team he had in place—about 35 men now—was working hard. He was brimming with confidence.

One reason production was increasing at the plant was because Booker was pushing it. He had become obsessed with yield. Part of how a distillery's efficiency—and success—is measured is based on how many gallons of whiskey the distiller can get from a bushel of corn. In the sixties, the yield goal was five gallons of whiskey produced for every one bushel of grain. As time went on, Booker became fixated with that number, trying to figure out ways to not only achieve it, but to surpass it.

He tried to do this primarily in two ways. First, he paid extra special attention to the corn that they used at the Boston plant. In Booker's mind, a certain type of corn—corn high in starch—would yield more alcohol. Second, he closely monitored the alcohol vapors that sometimes escaped during the transfer of the stillage (the spent beer). After the mash had been cooked and distilled, the remaining grain, or stillage, was sent to the dryer to prepare it for sale to farms for feed. Booker believed that there was still some alcoholic vapor clinging to that stillage, and he made sure to capture as much of it as he could through a careful control of the still operation. Booker believed that if you distilled too fast, then too much vapor would escape, so he did his best to regulate the still and keep it running at a consistent pace.

The men in the distillery thought Booker was a bit bent on the whole issue of yield.

"We made it to 5 today, boss," they'd say. "That's a good day."

"Not good enough. We need to make it to 5.1."

"Booker, now, with all due respect, one-tenth of 1 percent ain't gonna change nothing."

"That one-tenth adds up when you're making as much whiskey as we are."

"Hell, Clermont only got 4.9 yesterday. We checked."

"We ain't Clermont."

One of Booker's motivations was certainly Clermont. An unspoken—and for the most part, friendly—rivalry had developed between the two plants. More specifically, an unspoken rivalry had developed between Carl and Booker. The teacher and the student sometimes locked heads over the issue of yield and which plant made the better whiskey.

While Carl was proud of what Booker was accomplishing, he, like all mentors, didn't like pushback from his mentee.

This rivalry came to a head one day after the first shift. Both Booker and Carl were standing at the top of Beam Hill in front of Carl's house in Clermont, and they got into it pretty good. What they were arguing about exactly, no one is sure, but the word is that it probably had to do with production and numbers. The two men started yelling. One thing led to another and soon a wrestling match broke out, with Booker and Carl rolling down the hill in a tangled heap of arms and legs. The fight didn't last long. Within minutes they had brushed themselves off, shaken hands, and headed home. The next day it was all forgotten.

The fight underscores the passion both men felt about making whiskey. Each one was proud and stubborn and believed that his way was the right way. Booker was probably getting ahead of himself since he was still a relative youngster in the world of whiskey, but in a short period of time he had developed steadfast opinions about things. Carl, with years of experience, also had his views on how things should run. Both men were united in one thing, however: they wanted to make the best whiskey they could and make it as efficiently as possible.

In the end they worked well together, pushing each other to be the best distillers they could be. Booker was always trying new things, and while Carl didn't always approve, he deserves credit for letting his cousin flex his creativity in the pursuit of more and better whiskey.

Some of Booker's ideas did indeed change things. One of them was cooling the beer wells with hoses that were hooked up to the outsides of the well. The hoses sprayed cool water down the sides of the well, forming a shield. This shield kept the mash cool and kept it from getting too acidic. This idea eventually led to a permanent innovation at the plant.

Booker also had a hand in stopping the rotation of barrels in the rack house. For years, Beam, like other distillers, had moved barrels from floor to floor, an exhausting and time-consuming practice that some thought led to better-tasting whiskey. (Whiskey on the ninth floor was moved to the fourth floor, where it was cooler, then moved back up to the seventh floor, where it was once again warmer. The result was supposed to be a more well-rounded whiskey.) Booker didn't subscribe to that theory; he thought that moving the barrels was a waste of time and manpower—time and manpower that could be better spent in other areas of production. So after years of rotating the barrels he put a stop to it, choosing instead to marry together the contents of vertical cross-sections of various barrels in the nine-floor rack houses.

Booker also played a role in the development of the palletized warehouse, a low building where barrels are aged standing upright on pallets rather than on their sides, as is common in nine-story houses. Booker and others thought it would be easier to move and retrieve barrels of whiskey using a forklift in this new kind of facility. He also believed that barrels standing upright lost less whiskey. Preheating the beer, another innovation, also led to a savings of time and money.

While he had spent barely a semester at college, the Big Man had the mind of an engineer and a natural affinity for numbers. He often challenged figures his vendors provided him. His son Fred remembers one particular conversation with a concrete vendor:

"You said I needed 500 cubic yards of concrete for the foundation of the new fermenter, but I did my own figuring and I think I only need half as much. Here, look at this," he said, producing a legal pad full of handwritten calculations that he had spent half the night working on, using an old high-school geometry book to guide him.

The vendor had silently taken the legal pad, studied it for a while, then reluctantly agreed.

One day at the distillery, Booker was finishing lunch at his desk when Cousin Baker walked into his office.

"Just the man I wanted to see," Booker said. Then he said, "I've been thinking."

Baker, his reserved partner, rubbed his chin and nodded. Another idea coming, he thought.

"Had an idea last night," Booker continued. "I started to sketch something out, but left it at home. Here, I'll draw it again." He grabbed a pencil, smoothed down the brown paper bag his pork chop sandwich had just been in, and went to drawing, taking pains to sketch around the grease stains.

When he was done, Booker slid the paper bag across his desk toward Baker. Within minutes he had intricately diagrammed a new way to control the flow of grain into the mash tubs.

"See, rather than drop it all in at once, this new rotating device will regulate it, slow it down. This way it won't all get clogged up. Save us manpower. Won't have to unclog things. We spend too much time doing that."

Baker studied the bag. "You thought about this last night?" he asked.

"Yeah, couldn't sleep."

Baker nodded again. Hell, when he couldn't sleep at night, he turned on the TV.

"Looks like it might work, Booker."

"By God, let's try it then."

"I guess we will."

Booker's "here's how it works now, but here's how I want to change it" approach to operations often confused his team as much as it impressed it. In the end, despite some objections ("That will never work, boss!") he always had his way.

Consequently, pipes were rerouted, motors rebuilt, and processes changed, all in the name of efficiency and ultimately yield. (Years later, long after Booker was dead and gone, newly hired engineers discovered miles of phantom pipes that ran throughout the distillery, often leading nowhere. When they asked the distillery workers what the pipes were for, they shrugged and said that Booker had them put them in. He was always rerouting, always thinking differently, always changing his mind on things. Rather than taking the pipes down, Booker said to just leave them alone ("I'll think of a way to use them someday.").

All these ideas and every one-tenth of a gallon helped, because bourbon was in higher demand than ever. Thanks in part to the continued popularity of the cocktail party, and the two-heck-let's-have-three-drinks business lunch, sales of the whiskey were officially in orbit. Leading the way was the ever-present bottle of Jim Beam Bourbon, which celebrated the filling of its one-millionth barrel of bourbon in June of 1965 under the proud and watchful eyes of T. Jeremiah, Carl, and Booker Noe.

Beam wasn't the only bourbon on fire, though: according to the Bourbon Institute (now the Distilled Spirits Council), between 1958 and 1968 sales of the brown liquor grew from 25 million to 32 million cases a year. The institute's report stated, "Over the last 10-year period, bourbon sales enjoyed its greatest period of growth. In 1962, bourbon moved into first place in national popularity, maintaining a steady lead of 16 million cases over the most popular import—scotch whiskey."

The whiskey had gotten an additional boost in 1964, when the U.S. Congress had recognized bourbon as America's native spirit. Bourbon was now more than a special drink: It was officially a respected part of our country. Imbibing consumers could now feel that they were doing their patriotic duty with every glass they downed. Life for a bourbon distiller was good.

To help accommodate this surging consumer demand, Beam offered a number of brands of various proofs and ages. In addition to Jim Beam Bourbon, the company also offered the venerable Old Tub, as well as Beam's Choice and Bonded Beam. Despite these brands, Jim Beam Bourbon remained the crown jewel of the company. Attempts to diversify notwithstanding, in the sixties Jim Beam was essentially a one-brand company.

A new industry emphasis on marketing helped fuel the bourbon boom. Madison Avenue, recognizing a younger, more affluent consumer, began to shift its message from "good ole bourbon and branch, the drink of the South," to a sleeker, more contemporary one. Bourbon was now aspirational, the drink you enjoyed when you'd made it, the drink you wanted to be heard asking for and seen sipping. Status had never tasted so good. Print ads in *Life*, *Time*, and even the scandalous *Playboy* magazine depicted suave, attractive drinkers unwinding after another successful day in the corner office. Celebrities such as Sean Connery, holding a rocks glass full of bourbon, began appearing in Beam print ads. If James Bond is drinking bourbon, well then, so am I, the newly promoted district manager of Woolworth's in Cleveland would decide when approaching the liquor aisle of his grocery store. We're both worth it.

While Jim Beam marketed heavily to this new consumer, it continued to tout its heritage as well. Since its lineage was longer than all of its competitors, and the Beam name stronger and more recognizable, it wisely chose not to abandon its roots. Its long heritage was an advantage—an advantage it had every intention of leveraging. Consequently, ads featuring Carl, Booker, Baker, and David Beam (Carl's youngest son), along with a beaming Uncle Jere, in various poses at the distillery— studiously examining the grains before boiling, standing before a well full, presumably, of Kentucky's famous limestone water, fishing together in a pond on the distillery grounds as one big happy family—began appearing in magazines.

In these ads (often in the background, dwarfing his relatives) was a smiling and friendly-looking Booker Noe, hands crossed politely in front of him, eyes bemused.

While others in the family could take or leave the attention, Booker went on record as saying he didn't mind it. His feeling was, hell, if it helps sell bourbon and they spell my name right, I don't have a problem with it. Take all the pictures you damn want.

It was no secret that Booker was comfortable in the spotlight. He was used to it. Having people recognize him and point him out was second nature to him. From the time he was a boy he had been singled out. His size, his dancing, his football playing, his skill with a shot gun, his parties: they all ensured that. He expected attention. His ease and willingness about being the face of the company did not go unnoticed in the marketing department at Beam. Memos were written regarding Booker's role as a potential spokesperson and filed away for future use.

Cousin Carl and his boys, David and Baker, shunned the spotlight; Baker in particular. As hardworking and as low key as his father, Baker was the polar opposite of his older cousin Booker. Thin, wiry, and with a head full of jet-black hair, Baker had steadily worked his way up the chain at Clermont. Starting as an hourly wage employee in the labor pool raking leaves, he had become irreplaceable at the world's largest bourbon distillery and his father's right-hand man. While he tolerated the attention that came with his last name, he was more comfortable with a wrench and a flashlight fixing what needed to be fixed so that the bourbon kept flowing. For years Baker was the ying to Booker's yang, an understated version of Booker and a steady and reliable presence at Beam as well as in Booker's career.

The Distillery

- *Fermenting room.* A large building with 19 fermenting vats inside of it. This is where the special Beam family yeast is added. The yeast turns the sugar in the mash into alcohol. The mash sits in the vats for a few days, until it starts to bubble.

- *Distillery.* Ground zero, where it all happens. After it's been fermented, the mash is taken and run through a column still, which is close to 200 degrees on the inside. The heat turns the alcohol into a gas, or vapor. This vapor is then condensed back into a liquid. This newly distilled spirit is called low wine. Since the low wine still has a lot of impurities in it, it is then run through something called the doubler, which is really just another still (though often it looks more like a pot). This still produces something called high wine. High wine is colorless and looks like water. Commonly known as white dog, it's drinkable, and it's what whiskey used to look and taste like 200 years ago when Booker's great-great-great-grandfather Jacob sold it.

- *Cistern room*. This is where the white dog is poured into new American-oak barrels, which by law can only be used once. These barrels are burned or charred on the inside. Beam's bourbons get all of their color and a lot of their final taste and aroma from these barrels. When Beam is done with the barrels they are sold to scotch and tequila distilleries. The bourbon goes into the barrel at about 125 proof. It's cut a little with water to get it down to that level.

- *Rack house*. After the cistern room, the barrels are sent off to grow up in the rack houses. These storage facilities are about nine stories high. This is where the bourbon is aged. The nine-story houses aren't heated or air conditioned and the barrels aren't rotated. The barrels are simply left alone so that nature can do its work. Between its Clermont and its Boston plants, Beam has about 1.9 million barrels aging at any one time.

- *Dump room*. After the bourbon is done aging (anywhere from four to nine years), it is retrieved. The bourbon is dumped out of the barrels and married together.

(continued)

(*continued*)

- *Bottling line*. The last stop before shipment, Beam's bottling line is state-of-the-art, bottling anywhere from 30 to 300 bottles a minute, depending on the brand.

8

Dark Clouds on the Horizon

A pril 3, 1974, was a warm and windy day in Boston, Kentucky. The skies were partly cloudy, the sun sliding in and out. Warehouse supervisor Johnny Hibbs sniffed rain in the air as he made his way over to Booker's office for the end-of-day whiskey tasting. This was a common occurrence at the plant; when the first shift ended, a handful of Booker's boys would congregate around a table to taste test samples of bourbon. These tastings often morphed into small parties, as the workers—in no particular rush to get home to wives, children, and chores—pulled up chairs to taste whiskey while shooting the breeze. More often than not Booker had some food to share: blue gill he'd caught or a pigeon he'd shot the weekend before.

As Johnny hurried across the distillery grounds, he took one last glance up at the sky, noticed that the sun was gone and the wind had picked up, then opened the door to Booker's office. The Big Man had been in a surly mood of late. Chicago had been calling and pestering him, about exactly what, Johnny wasn't sure, though he thought it might have something to do with capacity and sales.

This afternoon the Big Man was in fine form, however, laughing and trading insults with his team. Johnny pulled up a chair and took one last look out of the window (boy those clouds are moving fast), then turned his attention to the center of attention, Booker Noe.

Surrounded by small, clear, four-ounce bottles of unlabeled whiskey, he was arguing with another worker over a bet concerning catfish.

"I caught six of them, Booker, so you owe me. You said I wouldn't catch any in that creek."

"I don't owe you nothing until I see proof. I need *documentation*."

"What do you want, damn birth certificates?"

The room erupted in laughter and small glasses were handed out to the four or five men in the cramped room.

"I need to see some pictures of you holding those damn fish is what I need."

"Hell, Booker, I ain't got time to take no pictures of fish. I'm too busy catching them."

"Documentation. My damn birth certificate says I wasn't born yesterday."

More hooting and hollering.

"All right now, settle down. We got work to do," Booker said.

The Big Man brought a small glass half full of unaged green whiskey—white dog, clear as water—up to his nose and closed his eyes. The room fell quiet. Booker was tasting. This particular bourbon was standard Beam mash bill.

All eyes were on him as he gave his glass a swirl before plunging his nose into the glass and breathing deeply. Then he took one sip and began working it around the inside of his mouth, his jaw moving every which way. He called this the Kentucky Chew.

Over the years, Booker had earned the reputation of having one of the best palates in the business. With a sip or two, he could identify the age—most often right down to the month— and proof of almost any bourbon. His men had found that out the hard way; more than a few of them had lost good money betting against his palate. Booker loved being tested, and as a result won a fair share of pocket cash.

Booker took one more drink, then put his glass down, wiping his mouth with the back of his hand. "This one's a little off," he said, shaking his head.

"Bust head?" someone asked. Bust head was a term Booker gave overly green whiskey. If you drank too much of it, there was a solid chance you were going to have a busted head in the morning.

"Naw, it's better than that. But it still ain't there yet. "Red-line it," he said.

When Booker thought a bourbon was off, it was flagged, or red-lined, before it went into a barrel for aging. This meant that years later, when the bourbon was ready to be bottled and shipped, Booker and his team would taste it again to make sure that whatever kinks it possessed during its infancy had been worked out in the aging process. If it still didn't taste right at the second tasting, the barrel was set aside and more often than not dumped out.

"What do you boys think?" Booker said, passing the glass on.

The others took their turns with the spirit, handing the glass back and forth, sniffing and sipping. Hell, it tastes just fine to me, Johnny Hibbs thought. He was never sure exactly what Booker looked for when he was tasting white dog, but he knew better than to say anything. Booker's nose and mouth were money. No point arguing.

"Yeah, a little off, I guess," he said as passed the glass on to man next to him.

Booker drank some water, then opened a half-pint of red, or aged, whiskey. While the focus of his afternoon tests was primarily white dog, he often tasted whiskey that had just come out of the barrel to make sure it was worthy of being bottled.

"We red-lined that one four years ago," Johnny reminded him.

"I know that," Booker said, pouring a short glass. He took a sip, then chewed on it, his jaw moving sideways and then up and down.

"This one tastes fine. More than fine. Grew up nice. Seal of approval," he said.

As Booker took another drink of water to readjust his taste buds, he and the others in the room had no idea that an EF5 tornado was rampaging across Kentucky, coming up from the

South like a mad bull, killing and destroying everything in its wide path.

As Booker lifted the new glass to his lips, Johnny Hibbs took one last look out the window, and saw that it was black as night.

"Goddamn," he thought.

When the tornado hit the plant, the men in the room didn't really hear it. Booker's office was located in the same building as the distillery, next door to the dryer house, and the sounds of the various pumps and motors drowned out the roars of the monster storm. The office shook momentarily, the lights flickered, but Booker continued with his tasting. It wasn't until they finished sampling a third whiskey and the rain had stopped that they thought to go outside to check on things.

What they saw astonished them.

The twister had run just north of the office they had been sitting in, plowing its way toward the rack houses at the back of the property.

Up ahead, they saw the escalator—a 60-foot-tall, vertical barrel-lifting machine—lying on the ground.

"Holy God," someone said.

"Johnny, go get my truck," Booker said, throwing him the keys.

As the men drove around the grounds they saw the extent of the damage. Trees down, debris everywhere. Five rack houses were missing roofs, and one rack house, well, it was gone entirely.

The men stopped and got out of the truck. Where rack house J had once been was now a huge pile of leaking, cracked barrels.

"J is gone," Johnny said. He swallowed hard. He had been in that rack house just a few hours before.

"It must have exploded," Booker said. "Look, there's part of the roof way over there."

The men all stood quiet, taking in the scene, thanking God and/or their lucky stars. Then Booker slapped Johnny on the back and broke the silence. "If that twister had decided to make a left turn, we'd all be in that pile, but we don't have time to think about that now. We'll reflect later. Right now, we got to go check on everyone, make sure they're okay, and then get to work. We got a damn mess on our hands."

Close to 5,000 barrels of good Beam bourbon were destroyed in the tornado, which was just part of a super cell of storms that pummeled the Commonwealth that day. More than 70 people were killed and more than $100 million dollars in damage was caused in one of the most turbulent days in Kentucky history.

The Kentucky tornado of '74 served as an ominous and symbolic sign of things to come for Beam and bourbon. While Booker, Johnny, and the others set about repairing their distillery, another storm was already roaring across the landscape, threatening the very foundation of the industry.

Johnny was right: Those phone calls Booker had been getting from Chicago were indeed regarding sales. Slowing sales. After years of growth, bourbon was facing tornado-force headwinds.

After reaching new highs in 1970, sales of bourbon had hit a wall, the start of a long, 20-year decline. As Booker said, they had a damn mess on their hands. Vodka, a word you didn't dare to utter around Booker, was partly to blame.

More and more consumers were giving it a try, and for reasons the Kentucky distillers couldn't fathom, they were liking the clear, odorless liquid. This turn toward lighter drinks also included a desire for sweeter drinks, including rum, and later, wine coolers.

Dramatic cultural changes also had a negative impact. While bourbon had survived, even thrived, during the turbulent sixties, sex, drugs, and rock and roll had finally caught up with America's native spirit, relegating the whiskey to has-been status. Bourbon was now the establishment drink, something your "America, love it or leave it" grandfather might order at a chamber of commerce fundraiser. Manhattans and Old Fashioneds were for your great aunt, the one who complained about long-haired hippies and barefoot peaceniks. The names of the bourbons—*Old* Granddad, *Old* Crow, *Old* Taylor, *Old* Fitzgerald, *Old* Charter House, and the like certainly didn't help. Everything about bourbon was suddenly *old*.

Compounding the situation was the fact that distillers had too much inventory put away. During the go-go sixties, they had ignored some of the warning signs and continued to pump out a staggering and steady volume of bourbon. Across Kentucky, more and more rack houses went up and more and more barrels went into them. Over at Beam, the Boston plant was going full throttle, making whiskey that fewer and fewer people were buying.

In short, Jim Beam and the other distillers had failed to see the storm coming, and as a result were forced to spend the next two decades repairing the damage.

The Tornado of 1974.

The tornado that hit the Boston distillery was a part of one of the most violent days in weather history. One of the 148 recorded tornadoes to touch down across 13 states ranging from the Great Lakes to the Southeast in a 16-hour period, this supercell of tornadoes would kill 330 people. In Kentucky, 77 people were killed and the town of Brandenburg devastated. Booker and his distillery were lucky. No one was harmed at the plant, though more than 5,000 barrels, as well as one rack house, were destroyed. Eyewitnesses reported seeing barrels of Jim Beam Bourbon flying through the air, some landing hundreds of yards away from the destroyed rack house.

CHAPTER 9

The Party's Just Getting Started

In the same year that the tornado hit the Boston plant, Booker created his own storm with the media. In an interview with the *Chicago Tribune,* his response to a question about the surging popularity of vodka was simple and from the gut.

"How can anyone drink that stuff? It don't taste and it don't smell."

Booker then went on to give a spirited defense of bourbon, offering the reporter at his kitchen table a snort. "Taste that," he said, handing her a glass. "That's got taste."

Booker's argument fell on deaf ears, however. While the reporter was sympathetic to Booker, seemingly agreeing with him, she concluded her widely read piece (headlined "Bourbon Folks Don't Mix with the Vodka Crowd") by writing, "Taste is out. America doesn't want anything that perks up the taste buds."

Words like that were a dagger in the heart of the Big Man, who based his life around making a whiskey with a distinct and robust taste and aroma. Yet the numbers bore her out: by the mid-seventies, vodka was officially the number-one consumed spirit in America.

As sales of bourbon continued to slide year after year, Beam and the other distillers were deer-in-the-headlights confused, powerless to stop it. The moves they did make, such as cutting the price of their whiskey, ended up hurting more than helping. The stuff was now old *and* cheap, perfect for men on a budget. ("Hey, I got my social security check today. Think I'm going buy a bottle of bourbon.")

In response, a number of distilleries desperately expanded their portfolios, offering flavored vodkas and cordials, hoping to keep up with the changing times. While Beam also produced flavored vodkas (despite Booker's position), its overall focus remained bourbon. Beam made bourbon; it was as simple as that. (America, love it or leave it!)

Leading the bourbon defense was none other than Booker Noe himself, now the official master distiller for Jim Beam Brands. (Booker had been named master distiller of the Boston plant in 1960.) Cousin Carl had retired in 1974, leaving Booker to run the whole show from Plant Number Two. Baker was put in charge of Clermont, and together the two Beams soldiered on, cutting production and laying off workers as the siege continued throughout the decade.

Things got so bad that Clermont and Boston experienced occasional shutdowns. These shutdowns would last for months, with workers being either temporarily laid off or transferred to the other plant. Which plant shut down was determined by fuel prices. If gas got too expensive, then Clermont, which used gas as its primary source of fuel, was closed. When coal got too expensive, Boston, a coal-fueled plant, took a breather.

The company and Booker suffered another blow in 1977, when Uncle Jere died. The beloved and respected patriarch and popular spokesman for the family was now gone, leaving a huge void in the family, as well as in the entire industry. Since his retirement from day-to-day operations some years before, Jere had traveled far and wide, sharing the Beam story with anyone who would listen. In addition to losing the fine man who was Jim Beam's son, the company had lost its public face and voice.

After Jere's death and Carl's retirement, Booker stepped up and onto center stage. In addition to assuming the title of master distiller of the company (Baker remained distiller at Clermont), he was now the unofficial master of ceremonies for the industry. When reporters still bothered to come down to Kentucky, Booker was a must-see, a must-interview. When a local Kentucky industry group wanted to host a bourbon tasting or party, Booker was on the short list of speakers. With his "gravel dipped in honey" voice and six-foot-three, 350-pound frame, he was a presence and then some. Whenever he could, Booker would put his showman's hat on and persuasively talk up the many fine attributes of America's native spirit, guaranteeing its comeback with Churchill-like optimism and conviction.

"Taste that," he'd boom, holding a glass up high. "That's flavor! We ain't going anywhere."

Beam fared better than most during the bourbon downturn. If and when people drank American whiskey, they usually drank one of two spirits: Jim Beam or "that whiskey from Tennessee," Jack Daniel's. But unfortunately, they just weren't drinking enough of either.

Distilling and bottling for private label companies, the purchase of a food company in Los Angeles that manufactured a popular Bloody Mary mix, and a resilient porcelain decanter business helped keep the bottom line positive, however.

The decanters were a particularly effective shot in the arm. Since the mid-fifties, Beam had been offering ornate china decanters filled with bourbon to enthusiastic and passionate collectors. The business grew so large that the company eventually bought a glass manufacturer in Illinois to keep up with demand. Throughout the sixties and early seventies, clubs sprang up around the country with members buying, selling, and trading the decanters shaped like cars, banks, and even political figures. Some went for thousands of dollars.

While business slowed, things were at least going well on the home front for the Big Man. Son Freddie, an official college graduate (a college degree was something Booker insisted that his son have), began his long career at the distillery and Annis and Booker moved into the Big House on North Third Street, the last distiller to have an official residence on Distiller's Row.

Booker had long coveted the house. Like him, it was large and formidable and had a proud history. Every room had a story, held a memory. Suppers in the kitchen by the fireplace during the winter, listening to his granddaddy talk about his day at the distillery. Cocktails at six on the front porch, watching the cars drive by on Third Street. Parties in the backyard, eating country ham aged in the brick smokehouse. To Booker the house was more than a place to live; it was symbol of family and heritage, a testament to the past and a reassurance for the future. Like the Beams and the whiskey they made, the Big House was always going to be there.

Booker and Annis put the house to good use, throwing grand Kentucky Derby, Mardi Gras, and just plain Saturday night parties, whooping it up whenever they could. Booker was the force behind the good times, of course, drinking and dancing and eating his way into a sublime state. Everyone was invited to share in the revelry. Everyone was encouraged to stop by. The more the merrier. So what if America was no longer drinking much bourbon; hell, down in Bardstown, the liquor was still flowing freely, lubricating, inspiring, and encouraging conversation, laughter, and—in the case of at least one large middle-aged man—some serious jitterbugging. You got problems, well, put them over there for now. Here's a glass of Beam's best. Once you finish it, everything's going to seem a little better. Go on now, drink up. We got plenty. And don't even think about leaving the party early. "Where do you think you're going?" Booker would demand, taking back your coat and hat. *"By God, the party, it's just getting started."*

One of his parties became legendary. It involved a large group of motorcycle cops and not enough food. As his son Fred recalled in his 2012 memoir:

> *The Blue Knights were a club of policemen who rode motor-cycles for a hobby. Somehow Booker got hooked up with them*

at their annual get together in Shepherdsville to say hello, have a few drinks. (Knowing Booker, he probably thought you can't have enough friends who are policemen.) So, he goes over there on a Saturday night and one thing leads to another and suddenly he's everyone's best friend and suddenly he's inviting everyone over to our house the next day for lunch.

Fast forward to breakfast the next morning. Booker, buttering up his pancakes, casually mentions to my mom that he invited some people over for lunch.

"Well, how many?"

Booker shrugged, reached for the syrup. "Well, I never got an official count. I'd say three, four hundred."

My mom dropped her coffee cup. "Three, four hundred?"

"About that," Booker said, chewing. "Like I said, never got an exact count. But I think that's in the ballpark."

Sure enough, a few hours later, there were about three hundred motorcycles on our front lawn and parked up and down the side streets. The town was overwhelmed.

We had to run out and buy every piece of meat in Bardstown. Just about cleaned out two grocery stores. Finally, they said they wouldn't sell us any more, wouldn't be fair to the other residents, so we had to go to another town.

I remember Booker surveying the scene, his backyard full of partying policemen, sipping bourbon, eating beaten biscuits and ham, and listening to a local band he had hired.

"God damn," he said. "I bet I'll never get another speeding ticket for as long as I live."

They often took the party on the road. Trips to Nashville, Knoxville, and Lexington for ballgames and concerts were common. Wherever Booker and Annis went, they usually brought a posse of people with them and shared good times with whomever they came into contact.

Bourbon was usually at the center of things, of course, lubricating conversations, making stories a little bit funnier, dinner parties a little bit longer, and maybe mornings a little bit harder. Booker made a point of promoting his whiskey whenever he could, using these social occasions to remind his inner circle, as well as the new friends he inevitably made in hotels and restaurants, that there was really only one bourbon worth drinking and that was four-year-old, classic Jim Beam. He was always well provisioned on road trips, packing away a few bottles in the trunk to share at tailgate parties and cocktail hours at the hotels. When he traveled to see Fred at military school in Lebanon, Tennessee, he would cart cases with him to give away to the faculty. (According to Fred, those cases kept him from getting kicked out of the school.) He often bought rounds at bars for anyone who was lucky enough to be sitting there, or paid for strangers' before-dinner drinks at restaurants.

Every so often he would be forced to prove his loyalty to Beam and take a stand. In Knoxville he, Annis, and a group of friends once waited more than two hours for a table at a fashionable seafood restaurant. When they finally sat down to eat, however, they discovered that this particular establishment did not serve Jim Beam bourbon.

"What do you mean, you don't serve it?" Booker boomed.

"We don't offer it," the suddenly nervous waiter said. "But we do serve other fine bourbons."

"There are no other fine bourbons," Booker said, closing his menu. Then he said, "Annis, get your coat, we're leaving."

The famished group ended up eating at a nearby McDonald's, which, for the record, also did not serve Jim Beam.

"Sometimes you have to do what you have to do," Booker explained to an exasperated Annis as he bit into his second Big Mac.

Booker's "never met a stranger" approach to life was infectious. Any room he entered became a party. His personality drew people to him, and everyone was happy to be in his orbit.

His inner circle of best friends, while tight, was fairly large. Merrill Rogers, a boyhood friend from Bardstown; Jack Kelly, a Bardstown attorney who also owned the local watering hole, the Talbert Inn; his cousin Bob Noe Hayden, the football player from Springfield; Bill Roby, another Bardstown boy who worked at the distillery; and Donald Dick, a friend and basketball star from St. Joe's Prep. All of them called Booker his best friend.

These friends would humor him; they let him have his way and went along with some of his schemes. One afternoon he and Jack Kelly were sitting in the kitchen discussing life and death. (The pair was known for their debates and deep discussions about everything from politics to where the best piece of bread could be found in a freshly baked loaf.) It was during this particular discussion that Booker announced that when he died, he wanted to be buried in a cypress coffin.

"Why cypress?" Jack asked.

"Because that's what they use to make fermenting tanks. That's how I'm going out."

"Hell, Booker, there ain't enough cypress in the world for your coffin."

Booker mulled that over and got worried. "You may be right. I better start planning." Booker pushed out of his chair. "Measure me now."

"Say what now?"

Booker went into the living room where there was plush carpet. "I said measure me now. No use waiting. The way I live, I could be gone tomorrow. There's a tape measure in the top drawer. Go get it and measure me and write it down. I want to get the coffin size right. It would be a damn mess if it's too small."

"Booker, I am not about to measure you for your coffin."

Booker lay down on the carpet. "Just get on with it. I'll measure you next."

"Hell, I don't want to get measured. And I don't want to be buried in any cypress coffin."

"Well, I do! Call Merrill up, he's a carpenter. Tell him to come over. I can give him the dimensions."

"Damn you, Booker Noe." Jack knew better than to argue anymore, so he dutifully called Merrill and within minutes the pair was measuring Booker, who remained on the ground.

"Move over," Jack said. "I can't reach the other side."

"I can't move!" Booker yelled. "I'm supposed to be a damn corpse! Show some respect!"

A few minutes later, when Toogie Dick walked into the room, she stopped dead in her tracks.

"What on earth are you doing down there, Booker?!"

" Don't ask him, he can't talk," Jack said, measuring Booker's head. "He's a damn corpse!"

Of all his friendships, though, his relationship with Donald Dick stood out. Born on the same day, they were like brothers, inseparable for years. Both star athletes, they hunted, fished, and ate and drank together whenever they could. Their unique bond was solidified one night in their late twenties. After a few drinks, the two men, both recently married, promised that if something were to ever happen to him, the other one would look out for his wife. Booker's pledge unfortunately was put to the test when Donald suddenly died of pancreatitis. True to his word, Booker stepped up and made sure that his wife, Marilyn "Toogie" Dick, had what she needed to carry on. He became a surrogate father to the five Dick children, taking the boys duck hunting and fishing on weekends and including the entire Dick family on vacations. He even drove one of Toogie's daughters to the church on her wedding day. Legend has it that after they arrived in the church parking lot, Booker pulled out a miniature bottle of Jim Beam and offered the bride a quick snort before the ceremony.

"The first of many toasts today," he explained. "You want some?"

"I'm fine, Booker," the bride said.

"You sure? Might settle you down. Plus, these services tend to run long."

Over the years he was a consistent source of support for Toogie, eventually including her in many of his trips as a bourbon ambassador around the world. A marvelous cook whose fried chicken became so legendary that it was singled out as "the real Kentucky Fried Chicken" by the *New York Times*, Toogie owned a restaurant in town, Kurtz's, which catered meals for Beam-sponsored events in Bardstown. If she happened to have any extra chicken after the dinner rush, she brought it over herself to Booker and Annis to snack on late at night while they watched television.

Hunting, fishing, parties, road trips with family and friends to football games, working the day shift then coming home to fried chicken and *Sanford and Son* (the Big Man's favorite show), Booker's simple and predictable life stood in sharp contrast to what was happening in America.

The seventies and early eighties were a time of change in the country, with music, television, fashion, and Hollywood becoming more progressive and permissive. Women were finally taking their well-earned and long-overdue place in the boardroom, African-American and gay voices were speaking more loudly, and Americans' post-Watergate disappointment and distrust of the government was at an all-time high. Monster rock bands, such as The Who, the Rolling Stones, and Led Zeppelin, played to monster-sized crowds who used and celebrated illegal drugs, primarily marijuana.

Kentucky was not immune to these changes. Marijuana became a big cash crop in the Bluegrass State, with gangs such as the infamous Cornbread Mafia growing and selling copious amounts of it. Moonshining, once the king of illegal activities in Kentucky hills and hollers, now took a backseat to the business of pot, as musician Steve Earle's hit song, "Copperhead Road," would one day convey.

Through all these changes, though, Booker remained Booker, a solid rock, an unmovable object. As things swirled around him, as more and more Americans wore bell-bottomed pants, danced to disco, and experimented with new drugs, he remained true to himself and his upbringing. He kept things simple. He hunted and he fished. He went to work at the plant in the morning and came home tired in the evening. He partied with his friends on Saturday and went to mass on Sunday.

Rather than regard him as old-fashioned or square, people saw him as a link to less complicated times. To everyone who met him, he was a proud relic from another era, and rather than dismiss or ridicule his old-school ways, they respected and even envied him. Unlike so many others during that era, Booker Noe knew who he was.

CHAPTER 10

The Shutdown Years

In the bourbon industry, the lost decade of the seventies gave way to the equally stagnant eighties. In addition to vodka and wine, consumers were now turning their attention to newfangled single-malt scotches, nosing and sipping high-priced brands. Beer sales were also on the upswing. To the distillers it seemed that America was drinking everything but bourbon.

There were rays of hope, however; beams of light down the mineshaft. In August of 1980 the venerable *Wall Street Journal* ran an article about a little-known distillery in Loretto, a postage stamp of a town in the Kentucky foothills. The article

passionately touted the bourbon this distillery was putting out—
Maker's Mark:

> *Maker's Mark Distillery has made its mark by going against the grain. In producing its premium priced Maker's Mark bourbon, it continues to use an intricate six-year aging process and a small bottling line that are models of efficiency. It distills only 19 barrels of bourbon daily, compared with hundreds distilled by other producers. Its ad budget is a meager $1.2 million a year. But most remarkably, its volume of business has more than tripled, to about 150,000 cases a year, in the past 10 years, while the bourbon industry's sales have slipped 26%, to $23.7 million.*

The front-page piece was not only a godsend to the company—sales soared—but also served as a beacon of hope for the industry; America still had some interest in its native spirit. Maybe this small, handcrafted bourbon made by the Samuels family, the same family that used to live right next door to the Beams in Bardstown, was a harbinger of things to come?

While Maker's Mark cultivated a cult following, unfortunately the rest of the industry didn't seem to pay much attention to its success—or if it did, apparently didn't think it would last. Beam continued to plough ahead, offering a limited and somewhat uninspiring portfolio of bourbons that neither excited nor interested consumers or the media. Its attitude at the time—our whiskey was good enough for close to 200 years, it should be good enough now—wasn't resonating with the newer, more discerning consumer who was eager for different things and experiences.

Over at Plant Number Two it was business as usual. Booker showed up in the mornings, made his rounds, ate his meat sandwich warmed by a steam pipe, and ended his day, joshing with the guys as they tasted that day's run. It was a routine that bordered on the monotonous and Booker, well, he didn't like monotonous. But he, like the rest of company and most of the industry, trudged on.

Things came to a head in 1985 when the suits in Chicago decided to shut the Boston plant down for a while. No need to have two plants running, at least not now, they said. Consequently, Booker was forced to make some hard decisions about head count, which resulted in him trimming the team to the bone. When he was done there was only a handful of men left to oversee the rack houses and act as security guards. The rest were cut loose.

The layoffs bothered Booker mightily. These were his boys, handpicked by him, and he didn't want to let any of them go. He liked them and they liked him. Mutual respect and loyalty abounded. There was also genuine friendship. Booker was known to help out workers with personal loans for houses or cars. He even threw an engagement party for one of them, flambéing the steaks with bourbon and grilling them in his own backyard.

To be sure, he could be tough on the boys as well, and sometimes they needed it. When he got upset at someone because he thought he wasn't doing his job the way he should, thought he wasn't putting in an honest effort, he was known to get right in his face, throw his hat on the ground, and stomp on it to make a point. Sometimes after a tasting in his office, a worker who maybe had too much of that afternoon's white dog might give Booker a piece of his mind. Booker would let him have his say, then calmly stand up, jab a finger in the man's chest and loudly invite him outside behind the dry house "to continue this conversation in another form." Despite his age (he was in his fifties now), few if any of the workers took Booker up on his offer. They might resolve their differences with each other with their fists, but they pretty much gave the Big Man a wide berth when it came to fighting.

Some workers got Booker's goat more than others, and as a result he would have no choice but to fire them. One day he had had enough from a maintenance worker who had made a royal mess of a project that Booker had assigned to him. He fired him on the spot, telling him to clear out right away.

"I'd rather have no one do the job than someone who can't get it done!" he bellowed, throwing his hat on the floor.

Afterward, when Booker got home, he told Fred about the problem.

"Goddamn long day," he said. "Joe, he can't do nothing right, I swear. Tired of cleaning up after him."

"You let him have it?"

"Hell, I fired him, is what I did. An abrupt dismissal. Told him to clean out his locker and go on home. This is a business. People can't pull their weight got no reason to work here. We're carrying too many people as it is, according to Chicago."

They sat quietly at the kitchen table. Fred knew what was coming. He let Booker stew and think in silence before saying, "He's been with you a long time."

"That doesn't matter."

"Just saying, that's all."

Booker, he fell quiet again.

"He's got a whole bunch of kids, too. Four, I think."

"That not a problem of mine." Then Booker quietly said, "He's got five kids. Not that that matters."

They sat another minute or two. Then Booker pounded the top of the table.

"Goddamn it, go bring the truck around."

"Where we going?" Fred asked, even though he already knew.

"You know damn well where we're going. We can catch him before he sits down to dinner. Hurry up now, before he goes and tells his wife."

Fred and Booker drove to Joe's farm way out in the country, deep into a holler. When they pulled up, Joe stopped doing what he was doing and stood frozen by his porch. Booker lowered his window.

"Get to the plant early tomorrow and start in on that again," he said to a confused and slightly frightened Joe.

"So I ain't fired?"

"I tell you Joe, you're a lot of things, but, by God, fired ain't one of them. I guess I got carried away."

"Thank you, Booker. Thank you. I appreciate it."

"All right, then. Go have your supper now. And tell your wife hello." Booker raised his window, then glared over at Fred. "Now what are you laughing at?"

He fired another worker for drinking on the job. The fact that he was consuming alcohol during his work shift was bad enough, but he had been pulling on a bottle of Yellowstone, a competing whiskey, and that raised the transgression to a federal offense.

"Damn it! If you're going to drink on the job, at least have the decency and sense to drink one of *our* whiskies!" he yelled before terminating the employee—and hiring him back a week later.

Unofficial estimates had it that Booker fired and rehired just about everyone at Boston at least once. Some men stayed fired for a while, others for a few hours. In the end, he couldn't really pull the trigger on his workers. They were his boys. Family.

That's why the closing of Plant Number Two was so tough. Some of the men he let go he might never hire back, and this worried him. They had families to support, mortgages to pay. Any way you looked at it, this bourbon swoon was a bad situation. Something had to give and it had to give soon.

During the shutdown Booker kept up residence in Boston along with the skeleton staff to oversee the whiskey that was aging, rather than heading over to Clermont. Cousin Baker and his brother David had things under control at the Big Plant, and there was no need to go stepping on any toes over there. No sir, Boston was his home. He just had to keep busy and wait for things to change.

"Ain't nothing more boring than watching whiskey age," Booker was heard to remark. "By God, I hate monotony."

In response to this growing monotony, Booker got creative. If he couldn't make bourbon, well then he was going to try his hand at a few other things. He had some ideas to fill the time and one of them involved catfish. Booker, a lover of all things fish, decided that he was going to raise the perfect catfish at the plant and that he was going to use an empty fermenting tank to do it. These catfish would be perfect for eating, and quite possibly selling. Kentucky Bourbon Catfish, homegrown. Hellfire, those fish, they'll be delicious.

Booker filled a fermenter with warm water, then stocked it with fingerling catfish. Then he set about feeding them spent grain, commonly referred to as slop. This slop was in demand at farms around the area; it was bursting with nutrients, and Beam made a decent profit selling it, so logic had it that the catfish would go for it too and fatten themselves up.

In theory Booker was probably on to something, but the reality was that the slop sank right to the bottom of the deep tank so the catfish couldn't get to it.

"The slop is too heavy," Jerry Summers, an apprentice distiller whom Booker had placed in charge of the project, informed him one day. "If they can't eat, they're all going to die."

Booker was undaunted. A day or two later he decided that the best way to feed the fish was by turning the spent grain into small pellets that wouldn't sink as fast, if at all.

"Pellets?" Jerry asked. "How are we going to make them?"

"Why, with the extruding machine," Booker said.

"That's broken."

"By God, we've got to fix it then. This could be a new business for us. Pellet-sized fish food. We can market the fish *and* the fish food. It's worth a try."

Booker and his team spent days working on fixing the machine. When they thought they had it operational, they turned it on and fed in the grain. Rather than produce the desired pellets, it exploded, throwing grain every which way.

"Damn," Booker said sadly after surveying the messy scene. Then he told Jerry to clean up the mess and headed home to his supper. He would have another idea tomorrow.

"Got to keep trying," he said. "Nothing gets done unless you try."

The catfish enterprise was shelved soon, however, after someone accidentally raised the temperature of the fermenting tank to a high level. When Booker came in the next day to check on his fish, Jerry, the apprentice distiller, had the unenviable task of informing him that they had all died.

"Damn," Booker said again. But not nearly as quietly.

After some thought, Booker concluded that ham offered some possibilities. Next to fish, Booker thought the world of ham, and he decided that he could add some unique flavors to it by wrapping a ham in chicken wire and hanging it over a stillage tank. The steam off the tank would not only cook it up right, but it would give it a wonderful beer flavor.

This venture proved to be more successful than the catfish initiative—nothing exploded—and when Booker took the ham down, he threw a party in his office, passing out hunks of it along with some beaten biscuits.

His boys loved the ham. "Best ham ever," they said. "You've outdone yourself, Booker."

"I tend to agree," Booker said, cutting off another piece.

There were other culinary pursuits as well. Booker and the remaining staff raised hogs and chickens at the plant for eventual consumption, butchering and grilling the meat with bourbon marinades that Booker made in the kitchen he had put in next to the warehouse office. Breakfasts became big-time affairs, with Booker frying up dozens of eggs for whomever was there, offering them along with some of his special ham if he thought it was aged and ready to eat. Chili was also another specialty, with Booker ladling out hefty homemade portions at lunchtime.

"They used to call the Boston plant the country club," Johnny Hibbs would recall some years later. "Though it was probably more of a big restaurant. Booker was always making something."

When he wasn't behind a grill or stove, Booker kept busy fishing and hunting at the plant. He stocked the small lakes with bluegill and catfish, and the grounds were full of pheasant, pigeon, and deer. He kept busy at his personal wild game park, spending hours hauling in fish or stalking birds. He even went so far as to build a special pen in which he planned to raise pheasants for hunting and eventual consumption. He got pretty far along in the project—the young pheasants were growing nice and fat under his watchful eye—until one day a large storm tore through the plant, destroying the pen and liberating the birds. Booker was crestfallen, and after the rain stopped he spent hours racing around the plant in his truck trying to track his pheasants down, to no avail.

"An act of God," he mused. "You just can't predict them."

He also hosted large retriever-dog meets at the distillery. People would come from all around the South and have their dogs compete in various exercises to determine who was the best retriever of ducks. On weekends hundreds of dogs would scamper about the grounds chasing ducks while Booker watched with great interest and amusement. If the bosses in Chicago knew that their master distiller had turned one of their two distilleries into a large dog kennel, they never said anything about it. Booker Noe did what Booker Noe wanted to.

Ham, catfish, dog meets, and chili weren't taking up all of his time during the quiet years at Boston, however. In between his other pursuits and unbeknownst to all but a few confidants, Booker was putting his spare time to good use making something else, this time on the fifth floor of one of the rack houses. It was a special something that he had been tinkering with for a while now.

Plant Number Two was about to get busy again.

The Beam Distilleries Today: Clermont and Booker Noe Plants

Jim Beam makes 115,000 gallons of whiskey a day.

Approximately 1,550 barrels go in and come out of the rack houses each day.

Jim Beam produces between 500,000 and 600,000 barrels of bourbon a year.

Jim Beam has 1.9 million barrels in inventory at any given time.

CHAPTER 11

Mules on the Fifth Floor

Booker drove to work one morning with mules on his mind. By God, he thought, those mules might just tell me something. Or at least confirm a hunch I have.

He called Jerry Summers, the apprentice distiller, into his office and told him to find out where the most mules in the plant were and to report right back to him.

"Mules," Jerry repeated. Summers—young, eager, and college educated—had been hired to help modernize the plant and oversee the computerization of the distilling process. Though he had a bourbon background (his father had worked for years at

103

the plant), he was new to the business himself, and Booker's order, brusquely issued, confused him.

"Mules," he said again, still standing in Booker's office.

The Big Man glanced up from his paperwork. "What are you still doing here? You're not getting paid to stand. Go find them. I know they leave them on certain floors, they hide 'em. They don't want to be caught with them. So go on now and find them. Go."

Summers slowly turned and left the office. Standing outside by the distillery door, he scratched his head. He had been at the plant for a few months now and thought he knew it pretty well, but he hadn't seen any mules about. Chickens, hogs, pigeons, even some deer—but for the life of him, no mules.

Finally, he thought it best to ask another worker for clarification. He saw Bobby Hagen coming his way.

"Hey, Bobby. Do we have any mules here?"

"Who wants to know about mules?"

"Booker does. Wants to know where most of them can be found."

Bobby paused. "Well, in the rack house, of course. That's where the whiskey is."

Summers looked over at the rack houses off in the distance. "Mules get inside the rack houses?" he asked.

"Yeah, that's where we sometimes leave them. You don't want to be carrying them around, and no one wants to share one, either."

"Share a mule," Summers repeated.

Bobby squinted at young Jerry, assessing him and the conversation. "You don't know what a mule is, do you boy?"

"I'm starting to think I don't."

"Guess they don't teach you the important stuff in college." Bobby took a step close to Sommers and talked in a low, conspiratorial voice. "It's a small rubber hose, see. And people have been known to put it in the barrel when they want to take a drink or two."

"Kind of like a thief," Summers said, referring to the two-foot copper piping he and others used to draw whiskey from the barrel to test it.

"Let's just say it's kind of like an unofficial thief, if you get my picture. Used primarily for enjoyment and refreshment for the workers. Keeps the boys motivated. Say, how come Booker's asking about mules?"

"Hell if I know," Summers said, walking away.

Jerry spent most of the day in the rack houses, crawling over barrels, walking on the plank floors. He found mules here and there, but he found the most on the fifth floor, the center of the nine-floor rack house.

"Suspicions confirmed," Booker said, when Jerry reported back to him, "The fifth floor. I bet you saw a few shiny barrels up there too."

"Now that you mention it, I guess I did."

"The fifth floor," Booker said, leaning back in his chair and putting his hands behind his head. "That's what I thought. But I wanted to be sure." He fell quiet, thinking. "Now why do you suppose they got all those mules on that floor?" he asked.

Summers shrugged. Hell, a few hours ago, he didn't even know what a mule was. Damn if he knew why there were so many of them up there.

"Because that's where the best bourbon is," Booker said, answering his own question.

"Oh," Sommers said. "Guess that makes sense. The men are probably drinking that whiskey."

"Damn right they are," Booker said. "Damn right." Then he fell silent again and looked out his window.

"Excuse me, Booker, but is drinking at the plant allowed?" Summers asked.

"Hell no," Booker said. "They shouldn't be doing it. I aim to crack down on the practice one day. But boys will be boys."

Summers stood uneasily in front of Booker's desk and watched the Big Man think and ponder. "You need me for anything else?"

"What? No. You did good, though, you did good."

At the time Booker got the confirmation about the fifth floor, he had already been making something special at the distillery. It was a whiskey that was coming off the doubler low, at 125 proof, and going straight into the barrel.

He was also playing with the filtration process. Actually, he wasn't so much playing with it as just not doing it. This new stuff wasn't going to be filtered. Strained, yes, but not chill filtered. No sir, old school all the way on this one. Flavor, big-time flavor, was what Booker was after. And while he was at it, he wasn't cutting it with water either. This was the real deal, big and bold. He wanted to drink something like his grandfather Jim did when he was young. Maybe great- and great-great-granddaddies David M. and David, too, for that matter.

And now he knew for sure where he was going to age this whiskey. The fifth floor. Perfect spot for it. The center cut of the rack house. Right temperature, right humidity. Not too hot, not too cold. Put up a few barrels of it there, and when it's ready, dump it all together. Everything from one floor. A horizontal selection of barrels, not a vertical collection like all the others. Yes, sir, then we will see what we got.

By the mid to late eighties, as the Boston plant remained closed, bourbon was starting to show a little life. Not much, but the bleeding was beginning to slow. Thanks to a robust export market sales of Jim Beam Bourbon were on the upswing, and Beam was finally able to make a dent in its large inventories. Domestically, smaller brands such as Maker's Mark were continuing to gain traction, too. The mood of America was also changing. Ronald Reagan, confident and optimistic, was in office, the long-dormant stock market was in the early stages of a historic bull run, the Soviet Union was teetering under new boss Mikhail Gorbachev, and consumer demand for new and unique products, tastes, and experiences was officially in full throttle. The anxiety-ridden, downcast seventies were as dead as disco. Big things—cars, houses, hair, and business—were back.

Lucky visitors to the Boston plant, though they were few and far between, got a taste of big things to come when they stopped by Booker's office during that period. One day in 1984, one of those visitors happened to be Mike Donohoe, a rising young salesman from the West Coast. Donohoe was new to Beam; he had been hired just months ago and was taking the obligatory tour of the two plants to learn the process of whiskey making. Though he was a suit, he was personable and low key and had played in the NFL, so Booker took a liking to him and invited Donohoe to stop by his office at four in the afternoon to taste something special.

When Booker asked you to do something, you did it, even if you had played in the NFL. Donohoe showed up right on time.

"Come on, sit down," Booker said. "Got something I want you to try. Booker pulled out a pint full of a dark bourbon. The bottle had no label.

"What are we drinking, Booker?"

"Just something I've been playing with. Something I've been drinking. You know, one good thing about running this place is you know where all the best barrels are. Hell, if you can't get a good drink at a distillery, you're a damn fool."

"Thought you only drank Old Tub," Donohoe said. Booker's penchant for Old Tub, one of Beam's old bourbons, was well known.

"Would if I could, but we don't make that anymore. This stuff is better anyway. At least I think so." Booker poured a small snort into a glass and added some good water. Then he handed it on over to Donohoe. "Try that on for size, but sip it slow. Got some fire and kick in it."

Donohoe drank the whiskey and when he did, he tasted the future. "What is this?"

"Something different. Been working on it for a while now. Higher proof, straight from the barrel. Just like the old days."

Donohoe took another sip. "It's amazing."

"Damn right it is."

"How much of this do you have?"

"Not much. I got some barrels aging."

"Maybe you should make more."

Booker poured them each another glass. "Maybe I should do just that."

Throughout the decade, while Booker continued to perfect this special whiskey, others in the industry were getting creative as well. Sensing the time was right for something different, the distillers were finally stirring, waking up to a new world that offered possibilities. They watched with great interest as consumers continued to buy and drink high-end single-malt scotch, whiskey that could cost upwards of $100 a bottle. For years, conventional wisdom had had it that no one would ever want, much less pay for, a super-premium bourbon: the industry's consumer base—old and getting older—simply didn't have the money or interest. But the success of single malts changed more than a few minds. Why not us, the distillers asked.

Rival Kentucky distiller Ancient Age struck first, offering Blanton's: a single-barrel, super-premium bourbon. Packaged in a distinct bottle that captured its uniqueness, the whiskey was a modest hit but did not change the spirits world. Still, it was a step in the right direction.

Meanwhile, over in tiny Loretto, Kentucky, sales of the Samuels' Maker's Mark were still growing. Produced in relatively limited quantities, a fact the company promoted, it was developing a following that bordered on the fanatical, with new consumers finding and falling in love with it daily.

Despite these obvious trends, Beam continued to plod along. Though its portfolio expanded in 1987 with the acquisition of National Distillers, whose brands included quality (but hardly new) bourbons such as Old Grand-Dad and Old Crow, it was generally content to offer a relatively limited portfolio of bourbons—which included, of course, its crown jewel, Jim Beam Original.

While all this was going on, the Big Man continued to make and age his special, still-to-be-named whiskey on the fifth floor, giving it away to friends and family around the holidays or on other special occasions. Word was getting out that Booker had a special bourbon, and if you were good (and lucky), well then Santa might just treat you right come Christmas.

During the eighties, Booker's not-so-secret whiskey only furthered his growing status with his peers and industry types. His personality was as big as ever, his circle of friends widening, and his influence on all things bourbon growing. Quite simply, the Big Man was emerging as The Man.

Confirmation of his rising status came in the form of a 1987 profile that *Esquire*, the *it* magazine of the decade, ran on Booker. The article, part of the magazine's ongoing American Original series, included descriptions of Booker eating and drinking:

> *Booker gets to smacking his lips and belching some quiet ones. The smacking means Booker wants another snort of Jim. Jim Beam Kentucky straight bourbon is what he drinks, practically the only alcoholic beverage he's drunk since he was seven or eight . . . .*

And . . .

> *Booker's the widest kind of man; bald except for the silver sprigs of hay on the temples and out back, feet as thick and big as stumps, and a voice that goes deep when he eats.*

The profile, while entertaining, wasn't all that flattering, and the corporate PR people weren't happy with the hillbilly undertones of the piece. Booker, though, couldn't have cared less; he never even read it.

His boys at the plant did, however. A week or so after the article appeared, Booker walked into the distillery to find his crew sporting new sweatshirts that had Booker Noe, American Original printed on the front, along with Booker's face.

"Goddamn," Booker smiled. "I didn't think you boys even knew how to read."

Booker's profile was further raised that year by his appearance in a celebrated and widely viewed music video starring Hank Williams Junior. Williams had emerged as a star in the late eighties, singing to sold-out venues across the country. Booker's son, Fred, who briefly worked for Williams, had been urging the company to sponsor Williams for years, and after some debate the company finally had agreed. A friendship between Booker and Williams eventually and naturally developed, of course. Booker was a frequent guest at Williams' concerts and more than one time was asked onstage to jitterbug with the boys in the band. Occasionally Booker, egged on by the adoring crowd, would playfully stomp on the hat of a competing bourbon company that someone from the band had given him. After he had had his way with the hat, he would swig some Beam, shake hands with people in the first row, and return to his seat. Just another day in the life of a Kentucky bourbon distiller.

When Williams asked Booker to appear in a new music video he was shooting in Nashville, "Young Country," Booker was hesitant, though.

"What do I have to do?"

"Just have a good time. We'll give you one line to say."

"As long as I don't have to sing."

"I'll handle the singing," Hank said.

Booker asked Fred to drive him down to Nashville, and when they got there they realized this wasn't just any music video. People ranging from football superstar Walter Payton to Minnie Pearl to Gary Rossington from Lynyrd Skynyrd were also there preparing for the video. Even legendary guitarist Les Paul was on hand.

"You know any of these people?" Booker asked starstruck Fred.

Mouth partially open, eyes wide, Fred just nodded his head.

The shoot took two days, with Booker saying his assigned line, "That ain't country," perfectly each time. When it was over, Booker asked Fred to go out in the truck and bring in some whiskey for the wrap party.

"Get some Beam, and that special stuff too," he said, referring to the bourbon from the fifth floor.

When Fred returned with the bourbon, someone from Hank's band grabbed the bottle and threw down three sizable gulps.

Everyone was quiet, amazed at the consumption. Then Booker said, "I do believe that boy likes that stuff," as the room erupted in laughter.

Later on, the special whiskey from the fifth floor was also passed around. "It's like perfection in a bottle," someone said after he had a drink.

"Damn right," Booker said.

"What's it called?"

"I just call it Booker's for now. It's my personal whiskey, so hell, it may as well have my personal name." Booker poured himself a glass.

The "Young Country" video went on to win a slew of awards, including country music video of the year, further pushing Booker into the limelight.

Thanks in part to the *Esquire* article and the video, Booker was becoming more than just a distiller, more than just Jim Beam's grandson: he was emerging as a personality in his own right, a bona fide American Original. This attention wouldn't stop anytime soon.

The Fifth Floor

The importance of the fifth floor, in Booker's own words:

What I'm hunting for are the barrels in the center rows, the fifth story. The center cut is what I call them. I select from these central areas because I know from experience that the whiskeys in the seven-to eight-year range will be oaky and vanilla-like, robust but smooth. Not too much tannin, but lots of texture. Too much tannin will have it taste too dry. Hell, think of the center cut from a watermelon, that's the sweetest part. Center cut's what it's all about.

Huckelbridge, Dane; *Bourbon: A History of the American Spirit*, William Morrow, 2014.

12

Santa Claus
Is Coming to Town

The fourth quarter (October, November, December) for a liquor company is the most important time of year. Crunch time. The play-offs. That's when cases are moved, products sold. If you haven't made your numbers for the first nine months, well then, you have one last chance—the holidays. That's when people drink. That's when people splurge. Office parties, gifts for clients, dinners out on New Year's Eve. Booze flows through America during that time, a coast-to-coast river of happy hours and parties. For liquor companies, average years can become good years and good years can become great years if you have a blowout last three months. Bonuses are made and jobs are saved in October, November, and December.

Back in the day, the Big Eighties in particular, liquor companies pulled out all the stops in Q4. Marketing dollars that had been stashed away all year were now released for one last push. Billboards went up. Slick ads in slick magazines came out. Parties and local trade shows were held for retailers, bartenders, and distributors. PR teams flooded the media with press releases offering holiday cheer cocktail recipes—featuring, of course, their brands as the perfect ingredients for the perfect drinks.

Far away from the corporate regulatory eyes, gifts were also given by local salesmen eager (or desperate) to make their year-end numbers. Some of these gifts were lavish. Hey, you want that minibike for your kid? Well then, you need to buy another 100 cases, and I'll make sure your boy is happy come Christmas. Hey, you're not sure about that extra 50 cases? Well, we got four tickets to the Knicks-Celtics game, center court at the Garden, that says you are.

In 1986 Jim Beam Brands was looking to finish strong. But to do that, it needed the attention, loyalty, and appreciation of their distributors as well as key owners of bars, restaurants, and liquor stores. For years Jim Beam Brands, which had been bought by American Tobacco in 1967, had made a point of steering away from big year-end gifts, since they smacked of pay-for-play. It didn't have to play that game. Still, it wanted to send out gifts that made a statement to its key customers. T-shirts, flowers, and candy weren't going to cut it that year. No sir, that year it wanted something special, something that stood out, something that said something about who it was and what it stood for—bourbon.

When Barry Berish, CEO of the company, asked Mike Donohoe for suggestions, Donohoe remembered that special whiskey he had sampled with Booker a few years back.

"I got an idea," he said. "Actually, we've been thinking about it for a while."

Donohoe put in a call to Booker, asking him how much of that whiskey he had.

"What whiskey?"

"We tasted it, from the middle floors. I've had it a few times now."

"Oh, yeah. I got some barrels. I was getting ready to bottle it up, give some away. I do that every year about this time."

"Well, we'd like to give it to some distributors too. Make an impression on them. You got enough?"

"Yeah, I got enough. Mostly eight-year-old."

"That sounds good. You sure you got enough?"

"Yeah, I got enough."

The suits in Chicago, of course, had a motive beyond just showing appreciation and encouraging a preference for Jim Beam brands during the holidays. They had a much more important reason to be sending this bourbon out. The timing was right to conduct a very small and controlled test market of Booker's whiskey, that high-proof bourbon made from a select number of barrels from the center of the rack house. The idea was to let some people have a taste and listen to what they had to say.

"When do you want to ship it?" Booker asked.

"We want it in time for Christmas."

"Christmas? Then Santa Claus better get busy."

Donohoe followed this call up with an official memo to Booker, outlining his thoughts on the project:

> . . . *This gift will be given to numerous people with the understanding that if they are bourbon connoisseurs, they should not mix it. If they are not connoisseurs, [they should] please save it for friends who are. We are hoping that the retailers will come back and say this is a helluva bottle. If they ask to buy a case or two, we can tell them that it's not really available, but perhaps next year. If the response is good enough, then next year or the year after we can go ahead and make an extra batch. We wouldn't be counting on any profit from this brand for a few years to come, if we went in that direction.*

The first official dumping of Booker's took place soon after. Booker pulled out a handful of barrels aged six to eight years from the fifth and sixth floors (the sixth floor was almost as good as the fifth, he had decided) and married them all together. Next on his list was finding the right packaging.

"We need something that stands out," Donohoe told Booker over the phone. "Something that says this is different, special."

"What kind of budget did they give you?" Booker asked.

"That's just the thing, Booker. I don't have a budget."

"No budget, as in zero?"

"Zero."

Booker paused. "Well, that's quite a conundrum. Let me think on that awhile. I like conundrums."

Booker called around and eventually located a small stash of old wine bottles in the area. They weren't fancy, but the bottlers were basically giving them away. Booker took the whole lot.

"Old Chablis bottles?" Donohoe said.

"Your budget still zero?" Booker asked.

"Yep."

"Then you get what you pay for."

Once the bourbon was bottled, corks were put in and then dipped by hand into brown wax, which dripped down the sides at bit. Beam's legal department intervened here, though. No drippings. Apparently, that was a trademark infringement— Maker's Mark, which had actually supplied Booker with the wax, owned the concept of dripped wax. They trimmed the drippings off.

Finally, a label had to be created. After some thought, it was decided that Booker would personally write a short note to serve that purpose. Pen in hand, Booker sat at the kitchen table, pondered awhile, then jotted down what would become one of the more iconic labels in bourbon history:

> *The whiskey in this package is the highest grade bourbon made by me here at Jim Beam. it* is uncut and bottled straight from the barrel. My grandfather Jim Beam liked his whiskey from six to eight years old.*

---

* According to legend, Booker was a bit nervous when he wrote this label and forgot to capitalize the *i* in this sentence. It remains the most famous "typo" in bourbon history.

As a final touch, Booker asked Johnny Hibbs and a few others to help him create an old-time look by using a small hand torch to singe the edges of the label.

When the label was done and carefully put on the bottle, Booker's True Barrel Bourbon became a reality. Exactly 2,978 bottles went out across the country, each label signed and numbered by the master distiller himself.

The Big Man had his masterpiece.

Official Tasting Notes for Booker's Bourbon*

Formerly the private stock of Booker Noe, master distiller and grandson of Jim Beam, Booker's bourbon is selected from the so-called center cut of the rack house, where temperature, humidity, and sunlight combine in perfect proportion. Booker believed that the best bourbon was aged between six and eight years. The whiskey is quality screened to remove pieces of charred barrel but uncut and not chill filtered at its natural proof, distinctions that set it apart from other bourbons.

Color: Deep, rich, smoky amber.

Aroma: Big oak, vanilla with hints of caramel, smoky charcoal.

Taste: Complex flavors of fruit, oak tannin, tobacco, and maple sugar.

Finish: Clean, long, fiery and full.

---

*Tasting notes represent the general profile of all Booker's batches; each batch is slightly different.

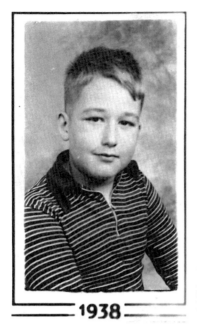

1938

Booker at nine years old. The pride and joy of Springfield, Kentucky. (Courtesy of the Jim Beam family.)

Booker (Second from left) was a prep star at St. Joe's in Bardstown, Kentucky. Playing both defense and offense, he was a force to be feared. (Courtesy of the Jim Beam family.)

The Big Man as a young man. Throughout his life, Booker was the center of attention. (Courtesy of the Jim Beam family.)

From an early age, Booker (right) was a crack shot. No pheasant, squirrel, or rabbit was safe in the hills of Kentucky when the Noe boy was around. (Courtesy of the Jim Beam family.)

Booker and Annis at their wedding in 1951. They met at a dentist office and were married for close to 50 years. (Courtesy of the Jim Beam family.)

Bourbon Men: Uncle Jere, (left), Cousin Carl, and The Big Man pose under the watchful eyes of Jim Beam soon after Booker joined the business in 1951. (Courtesy of Beam Suntory.)

Booker and some of his boys at a party. Wherever Booker went, he had an entourage of loyal friends with him, many of whom he knew from his youth. (Courtesy of the Jim Beam family.)

Cousins Baker Beam (front) and Booker Noe pose for an ad that appeared in a national magazine circa 1965. Legend has it that the boat tipped over soon after the photo was snapped. (Courtesy of Beam Suntory.)

The Beam "whiskey men" pose for an official picture in 1965 (Left to right: Carl, his sons David and Baker, Booker and Uncle Jere) (Courtesy of Beam Suntory.)

Baker, Carl, and Booker inspecting the grain. While Baker and Booker were always close, Carl and Booker had their ups and downs. Despite occasional differences, they respected and learned from each other, making the distillery a more efficient place. (Courtesy of Beam Suntory.)

The Big Man inspecting his (in) famous beaten biscuits at the distillery. Booker was obsessed with making the perfect batch. (Courtesy of the Jim Beam family.)

The Big Man checks on a barrel at the Clermont plant. Even after his retirement, Booker regularly visited the distillery to see his boys—and his bourbons. (Courtesy of Beam Suntory.)

When he wasn't creating at the distillery, Booker was creating in his kitchen, sometimes to his wife Annis' dismay. (Courtesy of the Jim Beam family.)

Hank Williams Jr. with Booker and Baker at the Beam distillery in the late 1980s. Booker loved music. (Courtesy of the Jim Beam family.)

Annis and Booker at "Bourbon Fest," an annual celebration in Bardstown, Kentucky, in the early 1990s. (Courtesy of the Jim Beam family.)

Booker sharing his wisdom and personality at a bourbon tasting in the mid-nineties. For years he traveled the globe spreading the Small Batch Bourbon and Jim Beam gospel, personally hand-selling his bourbons. (Courtesy of Beam Suntory.)

Booker, family friend Toogie (center) and Annis sitting around the famous kitchen table. A lot of bourbon was tasted at that table over the years. (1999) (Courtesy of the Jim Beam family.)

Booker in his "sunset" years enjoying the front porch at The Big House in Bardstown with dog Dot. (2001) (Courtesy of the Jim Beam family.)

Next to bourbon, Booker loved ham most of all. His smokehouse in his backyard was famous for producing legendary hams. (Courtesy of the Jim Beam family.)

Six and seventh generation. Booker and Fred in 2002. Booker was proud of Fred's accomplishments. (Courtesy of the Jim Beam family.)

Booker and grandson Freddie "Little Book" in the backyard. Freddie was the apple of The Big Man's eye. (Courtesy of the Jim Beam family.)

The Noe family in front of the Big House on North Third Street in Bardstown, Kentucky. From left to right: Fred, his wife Sandy, Annis, and Freddie. (Courtesy of the Jim Beam family.)

A bronze statue of Booker and his beloved dog, Dot, sits atop Beam Hill watching over the Jim Beam Distillery. The statue was unveiled during the annual Bourbon Festival in September 2005. (Courtesy of Beam Suntory.)

"Isn't it too bad your grandfather only left you money?"

~ *Booker Noe*

Some people *inherit* FORTUNES. Others are left huge tracts of land. But Booker Noe, of Bardstown, Kentucky was luckier than that. He inherited his grandfather Jim Beam's talent for making bourbon.

Today, Booker Noe carries on the 200-year Beam family tradition of bourbon-making with a dedication that could only be borne of outright love for the whiskey that calls Kentucky home. In

OKER'S BOURBON *nes straight from barrel,* UNCUT UNFILTERED.

fact, it's his own taste for singular bourbon that prompted Booker a few years back to start sharing a master distiller's secret with bourbon devo-

tees across the country. He calls it Booker's® Bourbon, and to some people in countries as far away as Japan, it's already made his name as famous as his legendary grandfather's.

> "*Where I grew up, here in Bardstown, there were more important things in life than the almighty dollar. We always placed a high value on family and on friends and on a man's good word. I feel lucky that my grandfather Jim Beam left me with an appreciation for all those things. Not to mention his ideas about making fine bourbon.*"

Booker's Bourbon is uncut and unfiltered, taken straight from the charred white oak barrels selected by

Booker himself. Booker's is then hand bottled and sent out to fine liquor retailers, where, from time to time, its price may climb above the $45 suggested retail, owing to its limited supply.

While some people do pay a premium to experience his bourbon, Booker Noe has yet to receive a letter complaining about the cost. It seems there are plenty of folks out there who really do value fine bourbon above all. Kindred souls who, when faced with a choice between having the best and saving a few dollars, apparently share Booker's sentiments. It is, after all, only money.

A few years after its introduction, Booker's Bourbon was supported by a limited ad campaign in select newspapers such as the *Wall Street Journal*. Most of the whiskey's early success was due to customer word-of-mouth. (Courtesy of Beam Suntory.)

Booker's Bourbon bottle image. (Courtesy of Beam Suntory.)

A view of the Jim Beam American Stillhouse, 2016 (Courtesy of Beam Suntory.)

Booker's Bourbon

Booker's True Barrel Bourbon was a hit with its target audience. Across the board, the feedback from distributors and retailers was very positive. Where did this come from? How come you've never sent this out before? Who is this Booker guy again? Is he that big guy we saw at the sales meeting? The guy with the cowboy hat? Can we have more? And most importantly, can we sell this stuff? Clearly, Jim Beam Brands was on to something.

The reaction, though limited to a relative handful of people, led to the logical next step: In addition to once again giving away the product to key distributors around the holidays, the company prepared for selling Booker's in small quantities at retail.

There were some hurdles to clear first, some issues to resolve. One of them was the proof of the whiskey. Some at Beam thought it was too high and argued for it to be reduced to a more conventional level. Booker refused to budge. This was his whiskey. This is how he drank it. They might be able to push back on other whiskies, but not this one.

In a carefully constructed and widely circulated memo to corporate he wrote:

> *I can't agree with bringing the proof down to 95–100. Dilution to 95 takes away ¼ of the body and character of the whiskey. It just tastes different. The rich color of barrel whiskey is lost and you won't get enough nose. The nose is very important to the enjoyment of fine whiskey.*
>
> *Let me know what you think.*

The memo made its point. The proof would remain untouched from barrel to bottle, falling in the 125 range.

Pricing was also a topic of heated debate. It's important to note that at the time (1987), a fifth of Jim Beam Bourbon was selling for between $6.00 and $7.00. Consequently, there was some thought that while it should be offered for more, it shouldn't be too much more. The belief was that after all was said and done, Booker's was still just a bourbon and people didn't pay a lot for bourbon. Wine, yes; scotch, maybe; but not America's native spirit, made in good ole Kentucky, which wasn't exactly France, the Napa Valley, or the misty and mysterious islands of Scotland.

A price of $19.99 was initially decided upon. Some thought that too high. They'll never go for it, they said. Senior executives, such as Rich Reese and Barry Berish, thought it too low. Higher, they said. This is special bourbon, Jim Beam's grandson's favorite whiskey, made by him with tender loving care. Aged in the center cut of the rack house, prime location. Not chill filtered. Higher proof. Nothing else like it out there. The price needs to reflect all of this.

The price of $39.99 was finally agreed upon. Some thought it was crazy high, others took a wait-and-see approach. Both sides agreed on one thing, however: Expensive bourbon was unchartered water.

Next, the handwritten label came under scrutiny. The marketing team didn't like the way the note looked. Amateurish. Homemade. Booker's handwriting was hard to read and there was the famous "typo" to consider. We're not giving this away anymore, we're selling it—and at a good price.

Let's clean it up. Bring in a designer and do it right, make it look high end.

You tell Booker that, Mike Donohoe said.

The marketing team paused, reconsidered. You going to call him? No. You? Not me. The members of the team then agreed: the handwriting was fine; no one's going to mind the typo anyway. It's just a capital letter.

Once the price was set and the packaging approved, it was time to pull the rip cord, let it fly. While Booker presented the very first bottle of his bourbon to his mother (she never opened it, and upon her death he retrieved the bottle), a relatively small number was shipped out across the country. No marketing was put behind it. No sales merchandise in the aisles. No pressure on distributors or retailers to buy it. No shipments to major chains. Beam wanted to keep the whiskey under the radar for a while and focus on high-end restaurants and bars. Beam didn't even tell its parent company about it. It didn't want too bright a spotlight on Booker's just yet. Spotlight means high expectations and questions, and Beam wasn't convinced this bourbon was going to make it. Plus, there really wasn't all that much of the stuff, so if it took off too fast and too soon, there could be supply issues.

The goal was to get it out there and get people talking about it, asking for it, and, with luck, demanding it.

Booker's bourbon, despite what others have written and said, was not an overnight sensation. People didn't phone their distributors begging for more. No one stormed Beam headquarters or flew down to the distillery in search of another case. For the first few years of its existence, it was a steady seller. It broke even the first year and after that it started to sell more and more. Whiskey writers and even some consumer publications consistently gave it high marks. Momentum with consumers and the trade was slowly being built. It was all good.

For his part, Booker was pleased and proud as could be. He gave out bottles to close friends and relatives, such as his cousin Bob Noe Hayden. He offered samples to anyone who asked about it and treated visitors to the plant to a drink in his office, always careful to recommend adding water.

"Bring it down to a proof level that you're comfortable with," he would say. "No one's getting any medals for drinking this stuff straight. One or two ice cubes, maybe. Sip and savor, that's what this is all about. Bourbon the way it used to be, the way it was meant to be."

Booker's bourbon was introduced at the right time. The confident and bold Big Eighties were rolling along unchecked.

Wall Street was still moving higher. Unemployment rates were dropping. Conspicuous consumption was in. People had some money and weren't afraid to spend it on quality, and even luxury, items. They wanted to treat themselves. They deserved it. Just as importantly, they wanted to impress others with their knowledge and their wallets. This watch was made in Geneva, Switzerland, by a sixth-generation watchmaker. He makes every single one himself. These cigars are hand rolled in Cuba. I got them when I was in Vancouver at a little store no one knows about. Took me an hour to find the place.

At tony bars and restaurants, the man-in-the-know would confidently order a Booker's, then patiently explain to his friends what the bartender at the Waldorf had explained to him just a week earlier on his business trip to New York: Booker's was the best. Uncut. Straight from the barrel. Second to none. No, it's a bourbon, not a scotch, the man-in-the-know would say. You should really try it. It's a little pricey, but it's worth it. Add some water, though. That's what I do.

Around the country, Booker's True Barrel Bourbon grew by word-of-mouth and glass by glass. Production was increased. More barrels were laid away. People who'd never drunk bourbon before were considering it, then drinking it, then ordering another. Maybe bourbon wasn't just for grandpa after all.

"Things are going well," Mike Donohoe said to Booker on one of their regular calls in 1989. "Your bourbon is selling."

"Happy to hear that."

"Won't be long before someone else comes out with another super-premium brand. It's going to start getting competitive. The game is changing. You helped change it."

"Had a lot of help. Have a helluva team down here."

"We know of other, high-end products that will be out soon."

"Yeah, I've been hearing the same thing. Parker Beam already has something out over at Heaven Hill."

"We're not worried. Know why?"

"Why?"

"Because we've got ourselves a secret weapon."

"Oh yeah, what would that be?"

"You, Booker. You."

14

Mr. Ambassador

The concept of a spokesperson, someone who represents a product or brand and touts its many advantages, enduring quality, amazing taste, and superior service, is hardly new. Spokespeople have been around for a long time. Celebrities, actors, athletes, doctors, authors, and experts have been part of the marketing game for years. Spokespeople are chosen for their appeal: their looks, popularity, personality, and credibility. What they don't know about the brands they're representing they can easily learn in a short period of time. Just read the press materials: Hold the product up high if you're on TV. Smile and say you use it, say it's delicious. Memorize a handful of message points and rehearse them in the limo on the way over to the event or the studio. Marketing 101.

When the marketing team at Beam started to get a few requests from distributors and retailers asking for Booker—the master distiller of Jim Beam Brands, the maker of this new high-end, super-premium bourbon, the grandson of Jim Beam, the guy in that music video—to come and maybe give a short talk about whiskey making, Beam was a little hesitant to oblige. Meet-and-greets at the distillery for special visitors and one-on-one interviews with writers in the comfort of his own living room was one thing. But asking the Big Man to put on a coat and tie, get on a plane, and talk at an event at maybe some fancy bar or restaurant, to smile and say all the right things, was another matter. It might be easier just to hire someone to represent this new bourbon, the thinking went. If nothing else, we could just use some brand managers. Media train them. Tell them what we want them to say. Besides, Booker is needed at the plant. Probably doesn't want to leave Bardstown. We can ask him, but we shouldn't get our hopes up.

"I'll do it," Booker said.

The fact that Booker agreed to be the ambassador for his new bourbon actually wasn't very surprising. First, he was used to attention and comfortable with people. Second, he was intensely proud of his bourbon and wanted very much for it to succeed. He wanted to do whatever it took to spread the word about his whiskey. He would preach the gospel and make Booker's bourbon his mission.

Finally, life at the Boston distillery—Plant Number Two—was getting, as he put it, monotonous. He had been there close to 40 years, and it was pretty much the same thing every day now. As Jim Beam Brands had gotten bigger, there were more people poking around there. No more rerouting this or that pipe, no more raising catfish, no more dog meets. No more cooking chili for his boys in the small kitchen at the plant. He loved every square foot of that place, make no mistake about it, but a little change might be nice. See the world some and meet new people. He would take Annis with him, maybe Toogie too. It'd be good to do something else once in a while, something different. The distillery would be there when he got back. He'd still come in most days.

Attempts to media train Booker were made, and predictably they went nowhere. Booker was going to say what he was going to say. He was going to tell the truth, speak his mind.

Booker never saw any point in the training and was confused more than irritated by it. "If someone asks me an honest question, then by God, I'm going to give them an honest answer. Tell it like it is. I don't need any practice in talking. Been doing that pretty much my whole life."

The PR folks, they got a little worried.

Still, the people whose votes mattered the most, the men in the C-suites, had the Big Man's back and were willing, even eager, to give him a try. He was authentic, knowledgeable, and personable. So what if he talked about his homemade cures for gout, or his disdain for vodka, or the time he shot that shark with a pistol from a boat off the coast of Florida, then hauled it back in his truck and grilled it up for the boys at the distillery. In a world of tired, cliché-riddled marketing speak, he was a blast of fresh air. An American Original.

And no one else had him.

To be sure, there were other notable distillers working in the industry. Personable and respected people, such as Jimmy Russell at Wild Turkey, Elmer T. Lee at Buffalo Trace, and

Cousin Parker Beam at Heaven Hill. And, of course, there was Bill Samuels Jr. over at Maker's: a rising star in the business, a personality, a force in his own right. They all had a presence about them, and all of them deserved and warranted attention.

But they weren't Booker. They didn't talk like him, didn't have that *voice* that was full of Southern thunder, a voice that could mesmerize, intimidate, entertain, and educate. They didn't have that mountainous *size*, that body that could fill a room or block out the sun on a hot July afternoon. Didn't have that inexhaustible *zest*, that thirst for whiskey, food, people—life. And finally, they didn't have that *history* that was forever draped over his shoulders, a cloak of heritage and pride. Six generations. A Beam. Each one of the others was a budding legend. But they weren't Booker Noe.

No sir. There was only one of those.

And he was about to hit the road.

One of Booker's very first appearances as a bourbon ambassador took place in Chicago in the late fall of 1989. By all accounts, it went off without a hitch. Booker told stories, signed a few autographs, and even posed for some pictures. It was a good start to the second phase of his career.

"Think we sold some bourbon last night," he reported back to the corporate folks. "They seemed to appreciate what I was saying."

That first tasting led to some others, and he found himself enjoying his appearances. Seeing new cities with Annis, and occasionally Toogie, meeting the local sales team, talking to bartenders and sometimes consumers. The crowds were still pretty small—20, 30 people—and sometimes they didn't listen to him as much as he would have liked them to (once they drank some Booker's they tended to talk loudly to each other), but overall he thought these tasting talks were successful. They were making headway.

When he wasn't on the road, he returned to his office in Boston to touch base with his boys and check on things. He was working on some new special bourbons that he was excited about, and that kept him interested. But these special bourbons aside, the light was going out for him at the plant. Getting a little dimmer. Things had changed. Being a whiskey distiller was all he had ever wanted to be since he'd turned 21, but he was over 60 years old now and beginning to feel out of step. The plant, especially the distillery, was now computerized, and while the process of making bourbon was more efficient and the quality better than ever, some of the romance and magic was gone. Booker wasn't about to spend the day staring at a computer screen.

His son, Fred, was working at the Clermont plant, paying his dues on the night-shift bottling line and learning the business from the ground up, so the next generation was falling into place. He didn't feel as needed in Boston anymore. His time as a distiller was coming to an end. He didn't necessarily like it—the plant had been his life—but he didn't like the idea of hanging on and going through the motions, either. This ambassador thing that he'd been doing, he enjoyed it. And it was important, too. People liked meeting him and learning about the family and about whiskey. He had a new mission now and he was excited about where it might take him.

The Rise of the Celebrity Master Distiller

The title of master distiller is exalted in the bourbon industry. Quite simply, it means you're the best at what you do. In the early years, the title and the responsibilities that came with it were ill defined and murky at best. Back in Jim Beam's time, it pretty much meant that you were the boss. Jim had held the title at Beam, as had Uncle Jere. Though both of them had spent more of their time in the front office, they knew their way around the inside of the distillery. Cousin Carl had held the title as well. When Booker was named master distiller, first for the Boston plant in 1960 and then for all of Jim Beam, there was no large ceremony. He wasn't knighted. As he once put it to a close friend, "One day they just started calling me that. I'm not even sure what the hell it means."

Booker's ascension in the industry, his role in the creation of the super- premium bourbon category, and his bigger-than-life personality helped define the position and title. Here was a real master distiller, right out of central casting. He had the knowledge, the pedigree, the charisma, the passion, the look, and the sound. In the late eighties and throughout the nineties, thanks in part to Booker, the title gained considerable weight. It was now clear what the master distiller was: he was the quarter-back, the conductor of the symphony, and the lead singer of the band all wrapped into one. In short, he was the star of the show and then some. Consumers and the media grabbed hold of the concept of master distillers and clamored to meet them. A bourbon manufacturer, recognizing this, did what it could to enhance the title and image of the person who held that position in the company. Bourbon manufacturers took master distillers out of the plant and put them on the road. In due course they became the face of the company, the men behind the bourbon. Living history. Celebrities.

As Booker's celebrity grew in the late eighties and into the nineties, so did the status of his fellow distillers. As noted, Jimmy Russell, Elmer T. Lee, Parker Beam, and Bill Samuels Jr.,[*] among others, all became known far and wide as masters of their craft. They were all special and unique personalities, and through various innovations and new products, they all played a critical role in the revival of the industry. While they were hardly the founding fathers of bourbon, it could be argued that they were the founding fathers of modern-day bourbon. And if a bourbon Mt. Rushmore were to be chiseled, they all would have their faces on it—and Booker's face may be the largest.

---

[*]While Bill Samuels Jr. never officially held the title of master distiller at Maker's Mark, he was very much the master of his special whiskey, overseeing all aspects of its production, packaging, and marketing for years.

15

Emeritus Man

The year 1992 was a momentous one for the Big Man. After more than 32 years holding the title, he stepped down as master distiller of Jim Beam Brands. Officially he was now master distiller emeritus, a fancy yet fitting title. He still had influence, still cast a very long shadow, still kept an eye on things. But he was now free from the day-to-day responsibilities of running the world's largest bourbon distillery. (Over at Clermont, Cousin Baker had also stepped down as distiller. A new master distiller, Jerry Dalton, a longtime friend and neighbor of Booker's and the first and only non-Beam ever to hold the title, was eventually named to replace them both.)

His reduced schedule at the distillery allowed him more time at home, time he put to use in the kitchen, much to wife Annis's dismay. In addition to being a distiller, Booker fancied himself something of a cook. His attempts at making the quintessential beaten biscuit became legendary. (Beaten biscuits went well with country ham, a staple in Booker's diet.) His grandmother had made them for him when he was a boy, and Booker spent hours trying to recreate the memories and the magic. He'd camp out in the kitchen for hours, his face white with flour and sweat on his forehead as he baked. Once finished, he would press his creation on to any and all visitors with a loud "Waddya think?" He was skeptical of the praise he inevitably received—these are great, Booker!—as in his heart he knew they weren't the best. A perfectionist, he would inevitably try again and again, leaving poor Annis to clear up the category-five hurricane damage he inflicted on the kitchen.

One kitchen episode stood out. Booker was trying his hand at cooking pigeon pot pie and regrettably left the pressure cooker on after he'd left to go to the distillery. A small fire ensued, and the house was inundated with the smell of pigeon for weeks. It was so strong that Booker and an outraged Annis were briefly forced to move from the house while it aired out.

"A waste of good pigeon," Booker lamented.

Annis returned the favor one day when making spare ribs. A wonderful cook, she frequently used bourbon as an ingredient or marinade in various dishes. One evening, finding her reserve of 80-proof Jim Beam depleted, she decided to give the new bourbon a try and liberally applied the 125-proof whiskey on the ribs, then turned the oven up high. Fortunately she was a safe distance away when the stove door exploded open, scaring the wits out of her and half of Bardstown. Annis learned an important lesson that day: Booker's bourbon was potent stuff.

When he wasn't creating in the kitchen, Booker grew an estimable garden full of the usual suspects in his large backyard: tomatoes, cucumbers, lettuce, and radishes, as well as a few rows of sweet corn. He was proud of the garden, as he was of his large brick smokehouse, where he aged and cured his country hams, reputably the best in Kentucky. The brick smokehouse dated back to Jim Beam's time and had been grandfathered in by the town of Bardstown, because by the time Booker moved into the Big House you weren't supposed to have one. Booker made good use of the grandfather clause by making good use of the smokehouse.

While he couldn't get the biscuits right, he more than made up for it with the ham—and then some. He'd get fresh meat, rub it down with salt, then lay it on an incline for a few weeks until all the natural juices were drained off. Next, he'd hang the ham up in the smokehouse and smoke it for a few days using green hickory wood, then leave it hanging for two summers. When Booker finally cut the hams down, he'd box them up and send them off to lucky friends and family, along with (unfortunately) his beaten biscuits.

The Big Man also had a pond built in his backyard, which he stocked with fish; catfish—and of course his favorite, bluegill— being the most prevalent. Initially he'd envisioned fishing in the pond and pulling out dinner with a hook and a line once or twice a week. He ended up doing it only a few times, though. Instead he grew attached to the fish, choosing to spend afternoons sitting by the water feeding them and admiring their beauty with his new grandson, Freddie Noe, the eighth-generation Beam who had been born a year earlier, and his beloved Dot, a precocious Jack Russell terrier.

In between cooking, gardening, and fishing at his favorite spots at the distillery, and bouncing Freddie on his knee, Booker was still making bourbon—still coming down to the plant two or three times a week to see how things were going, often bringing with him something to eat and share with his boys. Specifically, he was keeping a close eye—and nose and mouth—on his pride and joy, Booker's bourbon (the *True Barrel* part of the moniker had been phased out.)

On the days he didn't go to the distillery, his whiskey came to him. Regularly the plant shipped Booker's bourbon to his house, where he would personally taste it before giving his approval for bottling. More often than not, Booker included other people— distillery workers, corporate employees who were down for a meeting, friends such as Jack Kelly or Toogie, or son Fred—in these tastings. After swirling and sipping and asking for everyone's opinion, Booker would make the final call by either giving the thumbs-up sign or dismissing the whiskey with a short "Not ready yet. Send it on back to the barrel."

Booker's wasn't the only bourbon that had his attention during this time. The Big Man was also keeping a keen eye on something else—his special whiskies, a new collection of super-premium bourbons. He'd been working on them for years. Finally, in 1992, ironically the same year that he'd retired as the day-to-day master distiller, he deemed them ready for release to the world.

When the Small Batch Bourbon Collection, an assortment of bourbons made in relatively limited quantities and extra aged, was introduced to the market it was enthusiastically received. Booker's bourbon was initially the centerpiece of the collection. After five years in the marketplace it now had a small but devoted following (even guitarist Keith Richards of the Rolling Stones said he liked it), and Booker's drew that following to the other three bourbons—Knob Creek, Basil Hayden's, and Baker's.

The company had high hopes for these new bourbons, Booker's brainchild. Sales of bourbon continued to stagnate, and the only segment to show any life was high-end brands. Those bourbons, though representing only a fraction of overall brown whiskey sales, were doing well. Yet there was only a handful of premium brands to choose from. People wanted more, and Jim Beam Brands was ready—and all too happy—to oblige.

As with Booker's bourbon, not a whole lot of marketing dollars was put behind these new brands: just a few small ads in the *Wall Street Journal* and some nice-looking literature for the sales team to use. The bottling was unique, however. While the marketing team had decided to stick with the wine bottle for Booker's, the bottles of the other brands featured distinct styles that made them stand out on shelves and behind bars.

With the exception of the packaging and the ad support, Jim Beam Brands was once again counting on word-of-mouth, grassroots marketing to propel the collection into the consciousness of the spirit-loving consumer. And the main part of that effort was going to be Booker Noe. Jim Beam was going to harness his personality in a way it never had before. For the past few years Booker had been conducting tastings here and there around the country, appearing before small groups of people and leading them through samplings of Booker's, as well as Jim Beam Original bourbon. Now he would have more to work with: a whole collection of super-premium bourbons that he could share and talk about. Moving forward, he was going to see and meet the world on a much grander scale, spreading the word about whiskey in his own special fashion.

The Small Batch Bourbon Collection

Basil Hayden's: 80 proof

Basil Hayden Sr. began distilling his whiskey back in 1796, when George Washington was president and Kentucky was but four years old. His recipe, which contains twice as much rye as most other bourbons, delivers a distinctive flavor. Eight years of aging adds smoothness to the spicy character of the corn. This bourbon is perfect for those who are new to small-batch bourbons or who prefer a light whiskey.

Color: Golden amber.

Aroma: Spice, tea, hint of peppermint.

Taste: Spicy, peppery, honey, light bodied with a gentle bite.

Finish: Dry, clean, brief.

Knob Creek: 100 proof

Named after the hamlet in Kentucky where Abraham Lincoln was born. Lincoln's father eventually sold his farm for $20 cash and 10 barrels of whiskey. Knob Creek is a 100-proof bourbon and derives its rich flavor from nine years of interaction with the caramelized layer in new white-oak barrels that have been deeply charred.

Color: Copper to medium amber.
Aroma: Toasted nuts, woody, full bodied, almost fruity.
Taste: Big notes of oak, caramel, and fruit.
Finish: Long, rich, and glowing.

Baker's: 107 proof

Baker's bourbon is a seven-year-old, 107-proof bourbon named after Booker's cousin and Jim Beam's grand-nephew Baker Beam, a family distiller for many years. Baker's is intensely aromatic and flavorful, full bodied, and silky smooth.

Color: Warm amber, tawny nut brown.
Aroma: Fruit, vanilla, caramel.
Taste: Toasted nuts, fruit and vanilla, silky texture.
Finish: Sweet, smooth, medium long.

The Road Years

Booker said goodbye to his garden and his fish and hit the road in earnest soon after the Small Batch Bourbon Collection came out, taking Annis and a small team of marketing and public relations people with him. Not that he needed the company. Everywhere he went, he made friends: consumers, retailers, distributors, and the local Beam sales team. All were eager to spend some time with him, all wanted to be his friend and hear him talk about his passion and his new baby— the Small Batch Bourbon Collection.

During his early tastings he was initially paired with leading spirit writers, such as Paul Pacult. Erudite and knowledgeable, Pacult offered his opinions and insights into the whiskies. Since Pacult was one of the country's leading spirit authorities, his endorsement provided credibility to the fledgling bourbons, helping them get established. As time passed, Booker was paired with brand managers from the company: first with Tom Maas, a knowledgeable and articulate vice president of the company (and a close friend of Booker's), and later with Kathleen DiBenedetto, who oversaw the small-batch bourbons. On the surface Booker and Kathleen were an odd pair—she a city girl, he Kentucky through and through—but they worked well together, and Booker soon developed a genuine fondness for her as they barnstormed the country selling this new whiskey one glass at a time. Kathleen had had to earn her stripes with Booker, though, before he accepted her into his fold. She'd spent long periods of time working at the distillery under Booker's watch, learning the business from the ground up. When they traveled he subjected her to pop quizzes at dinner, testing her on what she had learned that day. These quizzes were not the easy true-or-false variety; they were difficult and tense examinations that often ended with Booker gruffly admonishing her to "pay better attention tomorrow." The message he was sending to Kathleen and the rest of the company was clear: If you're going to travel with me and represent my whiskies, you better know your stuff. Kathleen eventually did know her stuff and traveled with him for years.

The formal bourbon tastings they conducted were a some-what new concept in the industry. Frequently held at upscale hotels in impressive-sized ballrooms, they drew enthusiastic and attentive crowds. These crowds grew larger and larger over time, as word spread of Booker and his amazing bourbon.

DiBenedetto would kick off the proceedings with a detailed explanation of the proper way to sip a whiskey as well as some background on the small-batch bourbons. She would then introduce the headliner, Booker, who would lumber up to the podium in a suit and tie (and sometimes a cowboy hat) and begin a rambling yet fascinating dissertation on bourbon (There's nothing it can't do); his famous family (I loved my granddaddy); football (Watching it is almost as good as playing it); the best way to serve deer (They call it venison now, but I still call it deer); how he had lost his hotel room key that afternoon (By God, you would think they would give you two keys with what we're paying); an introduction to Annis (Hell, give her a hand, she's been putting up with me for 40 years. Where is she? Did she leave already?); how he hated airports (I'd drive everywhere if I could, but you can't drive to France. I checked); and how he enjoyed playing the jug on Saturday nights in his backyard with other musicians (We make fine music together). Somewhere in the middle of his monologue, he would lead the flabbergasted/amazed/amused/entertained crowd in a tasting of the Small Batch Bourbon Collection.

Some people, upon first seeing Booker in action, had trouble processing him. At one tasting, the head of a major distributorship in attendance turned to Beam executive Mike Donohoe and asked him a question.

"Where did you get this guy?"

"What do you mean?" Donohoe asked back.

"I mean, he's an actor, right? So where did you hire him from? He's really good."

"He's not an actor."

"Seriously, where's he from? He knows his stuff. How long did you train him?"

"He's our master distiller. He's Jim Beam's grandson. He's not an actor. That's Booker Noe. He's the real deal."

"Come on, be serious now. How much are you paying him? We'd like to hire him for our Christmas party. He's unbelievable."

After Booker spoke, people would line up for the Big Man's autograph and pose for photos with him. The lines would stretch over 100 deep, and Booker would patiently sign bottles, scraps of paper, and place mats, chatting amiably to each and every person he met, answering each and every question. Often people would present him with odd things, seeking his comment, opinion, or approval. Homemade green whiskey; old Beam decanters that had been passed down over a few generations; photos of grandfathers holding their favorite bourbon, Jim Beam; and, of course, bottles of Booker's bourbon to autograph. Everywhere he went people wanted to have some kind of special connection with the Big Man, and he did his best to oblige them all with his time and his attention.

Once the final hand had been shaken and the last picture snapped, he was whisked away by the local sales team for a very late dinner with a top account, where more stories and bourbon would flow and more people would be met. These dinners frequently ran past midnight, with Booker loudly holding court, much to the delight of anyone lucky enough to be there.

The next day he would often meet the media for lunch, where he would provide a somewhat modified version of his presentation to reporters or editors, leading them through a personal tasting of the small-batch bourbons, showing them how to sip and savor them the right way while reminding them how lucky they were to be drinking the world's very finest whiskies.

He also peppered these lunches with memories of his granddaddy and other stories from the distillery. Unsurprisingly, the media fell in love with him—Booker was a veritable quote machine—and glowing stories were written. As a result, his reputation with the press grew far and wide.

Some of his media lunches were more memorable than others. One in particular stands out. Booker was driving up to Canada to go fishing when PR man Jim, who was assigned to him personally, asked if he could make a stop along the way from Kentucky and have lunch with two editors of a daily newspaper. Booker obliged, and they arranged to meet at an upscale restaurant in the northern suburbs of Chicago not far from the corporate headquarters.

The interview was proceeding along just fine until the food came. That's when things went sharply south. Booker ordered the country ham, which was apparently not the restaurant's specialty. Seeing it on the menu, he couldn't resist. He also couldn't eat it once it arrived at the table. It was, as he loudly and angrily declared, chewy and flavorless, and all in all an affront to pigs everywhere. In short, the Big Man was outraged. You don't spit into the wind; you don't pull on Superman's cape. And you don't serve Frederick Booker Noe II bad country ham.

"Go get my ham," he said to Jim, the public relations man.

Jim stopped eating and swallowed hard. "What?"

Booker slid the keys to his truck across the top of the table. "I got a ham in my trunk. A big one. Go bring it in here."

"You have a ham in your trunk?" Jim asked.

"He has a ham in his trunk?" the editors asked in unison.

"You all hard of hearing? Of course I got a ham in my trunk. Big one. Was going to eat it up north. Might as well start in on it now. Go get it and bring it in here and we can all have a taste. I'm hungry. Go on now."

"Booker, I don't think you can bring food in here," Jim said.

"Why not? It's a restaurant. People eat food in restaurants, don't they? Last time I checked, ham was food."

"Well," the PR man said. Booker had a point. More importantly, Booker was about to blow his top. "I'll go get the ham."

After retrieving the ham from the truck, Jim was stopped at the door by the dour-faced and shocked maître d'.

"Excuse me, sir, but what is that?"

"A ham."

"I can see that."

"It's heavy," Jim said. "So if you don't mind. . . ." He tried to walk past the maître d', but the man stepped in front of him.

"You can't bring that in here, sir. This is a restaurant. We serve our own food here."

Using his head, Jim motioned toward the table where Booker—red faced, cowboy hat now on, arms crossed in front of him—was sitting. "You tell him that," he said.

The maître d' paused, took in the mountain of a man that was Booker, and reconsidered his position. "Right this way, sir." He then proceeded to personally escort the huge ham to the table.

With the meat safely in front of him, Booker went to work, carving pieces of it off and offering it to his guests, who raved over the taste. He then handed the waiter a plate.

"Sit down," he said. The waiter instantly complied.

When the waiter was done eating, Booker asked what he thought.

"Very good. Never had ham like that."

Booker nodded. "Now, go get the chef out here."

"The chef?"

"Go on, go get him. He needs an education about ham."

When the confused chef arrived tableside, Booker gave him an extra-large portion of his personally cured and smoked country ham.

"Eat and learn," he said. The chef ate the ham and proclaimed that it was good.

Booker raised an eyebrow. "Good?"

"He meant great," Jim said. "Didn't you?"

"Yes! It's very great."

"Damn right," Booker said. "Been hanging for more than two years. You can't serve ham before its time. You got to remember that."

"I will, sir."

"If you're ever in Kentucky, you stop by the house and I'll show you how to cure and smoke ham."

"It would be my pleasure, sir."

"Your soup was fine. Maybe you should stick to that in the meantime."

"I'll remember that."

"All right, then."

After the chef was gone, Booker asked other nearby tables if they wanted some ham. A number of people took him up on the offer, gathering around his table.

"People love ham," Booker said as he handed out generous pieces. "It helps make the world go round."

Another notable media lunch took place in New York City soon after the Small Batch Bourbon Collection was introduced. The public relations team had arranged for a lunch with two prominent spirits writers, one of whom was Gary Regan, widely considered one of the top bourbon writers. Lunch was once again proceeding nicely until Booker made the mistake of eating an *extremely* hot pepper. His reaction was attention grabbing, to say the least.

"By God, that is the hottest damn thing I have ever put in my mouth," he very loudly declared. He grabbed a glass of water and guzzled it. "Hellfire!" he yelled, slamming the glass down. "Give me some more water and call the damn fire department!"

The server, who apparently had recently graduated from the acclaimed New York City School of Snooty Waiters, rolled his eyes and asked Booker, not so politely, to keep quiet.

"Sir, if you can kindly keep your voice down. You're disturbing people," he said.

Probably not the right thing to say to Booker. He took the waiter in with narrowing and curious eyes. Booker was seldom, if ever, challenged. He was intrigued.

"Keep my what down now?" he slowly asked.

"Your voice. Other people are trying to eat. You're disturbing them."

"Disturbing them."

"Yes."

Booker fell quiet for a moment, contemplating. Jim, the PR man, held his breath.

"You know son, the only *disturbing* thing here is these peppers. They're too damn hot. In fact, those peppers are downright dangerous. They shouldn't be served here. You should remove them from the menu!"

"They aren't on the menu."

"But they're in my salad."

"I'm sorry sir, but I believe you're overreacting. Those peppers aren't that hot," the waiter said.

"Damn right they're hot. I can eat anything. And if I can't eat them, then I can assure you no one can."

"I think you're exaggerating, sir."

"Exaggerating? You hear that, Jim?" he asked Jim.

"I heard that, Booker."

"What do you think of that?"

"Well," Jim looked nervously around the restaurant, "I think we should get the bill."

"Exaggerating? I don't believe I am. In fact, I bet you $100 you can't eat one," he said to the waiter. To emphasize his point, Booker took out his wallet, pulled out a crisp $100 bill, and placed it on the table. "One hundred dollars," he said. "All yours for the taking."

The table, and half of the restaurant, fell silent. All eyes were now on the waiter.

"You don't have to do this," Jim whispered to the waiter. "You can just walk away."

"I will accept your challenge," the waiter said.

Booker examined his plate, located a large pepper, then passed it on over. "Bon appétit," he said.

The waiter cleared his throat, then carefully put the pepper into his mouth and bit down. A moment later, his face exploded in a mixture of pain, perspiration, shock, and fear. He yelled something indecipherable, cupped his hands over his mouth, and bolted into the kitchen.

Booker watched the waiter sprint away. "Well, well, well," he said. "I guess some people, they just have to learn the hard way."

There was then considerable debate with the spirits writers over whether the waiter had earned the $100.

"There's a possibility he spit it out," one of the writers said.

"That's a possibility, yes," Booker said, pondering. After more discussion, he decided to give the waiter the money. "Everyone is entitled to earn a living."

Chicago, New York, Seattle, Boston, San Diego, Milwaukee, Miami: Booker and the Small Batch Express visited them all, raising awareness about the brands as well as about himself. Everywhere he went he brought excitement, knowledge, history, and more than a little chaos with him. Most of all, he brought increased sales. After leaving a market, sales inevitably soared.

When traveling, Booker was no prima donna. Rather, he watched every dime of the company's money. He hated waste. And hated to be treated special. He refused to fly first class and refused to buy an extra seat in coach, choosing instead to take up half of Annis's seat—along with one-third of Toogie's when she was with them.

"We'll manage," he'd say, as he buckled his seat belt and the women groaned and scooted over.

Eventually the marketing team asked Booker to go overseas and spread the gospel internationally. Booker and Annis obliged, packing an extra suitcase and heading off, with Toogie tagging along.

One of their first stops was Australia, a huge bourbon market. When Booker landed, he was treated like a visiting head of state. The sales team and local distributor had gone so far as to arrange a red carpet and a drumroll greeting at the airport. Afterward he was escorted to a luncheon where he was respectfully asked to flambé pork chops using Booker's bourbon. A large crowd gathered around him as he poured the liquor liberally onto the meat. Within seconds he had created a significant firestorm, with flames shooting everywhere. Fearing things were getting out of control, he quickly handed the bottle to a local salesperson, suggested that the fire department be called, and grabbed Annis and Toogie.

"I believe we have an interview to go to now," he explained, hustling off as the fire raged behind him.

Later that evening, at a reception, the local sales team made the mistake of trying to outdrink the Big Man. This was a common practice in most of the markets Booker visited. Trying to outdrink the famous Booker Noe was something salespeople— mostly men, and many of whom were former college athletes— saw as a challenge. If they could outdrink him, or just stay with him drink for drink, they would have bragging rights—street cred—within the industry. Fortunately Booker never went along with the challenge, urging locals instead to "slow down," and reminding them that "this ain't a contest." That night in Sydney, however, members of the sales team were determined to put on a show, and they paid a big price. A number of them overdid it.

"They're going to feel it tomorrow," Booker said, shaking his head. "And maybe the next day, too. My whiskey is supposed to make you happy, not sick."

Booker's travels took him to Japan, another key market, as well. Years before, the Japanese had fallen in love with America's native spirit and sales of bourbon, particularly Jim Beam, were on the rise. Booker's mission in the Far East was to strengthen this growing bourbon base, as well as generate awareness of Knob Creek, Basil Hayden's, and Baker's.

His reception in Japan equaled his welcome in Australia. The Japanese were thrilled to have the Big Man in their country, and they showered him with attention and accolades. Wherever he went, people stopped and stared at the large American with the loud voice, this legendary whiskey man from the sacred land of Kentucky, birthplace of bourbon.

"Damn, if I bow my head one more time, I swear it's going to fall off," he said to Annis.

The food was something of an issue there, though. Booker, who could (and did) eat just about anything, had problems with shellfish. It didn't sit right with him. Unfortunately, at one dinner shellfish was the main course, and Booker, not wanting to insult his hosts, purposely kept dropping it on the floor.

"Damn, I'm all thumbs tonight," he said after knocking his plate over.

His understanding hosts would immediately rush another plate of shellfish his way, only to have Booker once again "accidentally" drop it on the floor.

"By God, it must be the jet lag. I swear. Downright embarrassing is what it is."

This kept up until he finally passed his plate over to Toogie and Annis and quietly ordered them to "eat the fish fast, before they come back." Once they returned to the hotel, Booker called room service and ordered two cheeseburgers with extra fries.

Paris was another stop for Booker and the team. He liked the City of Lights, and it liked him. Promoting whiskey—especially bourbon—in what is generally considered the epicenter of the wine world was a bit of a challenge, but Booker managed just fine, speaking not-so-eloquently through an interpreter at various lunches, dinners, and tastings. As they had in Tokyo,

Sydney, New York, and the other cities he had visited, people took Booker to their hearts and ate up his every word. Their reception confirmed what Booker had known for years: People are the same the world over. Doesn't matter where you are, what language you speak. They all want to hear good stories and experience new things. They all want a chance, an excuse, to have a big time. Treat them with respect, listen to what they have to say, and they'll return the favor.

Booker did his share of culinary exploration in France. Ever-curious about anything consumable, he was particularly adventurous there, sampling all the country had to offer. Of particular interest was the delicacy foie gras. Booker took one bite and fell deeply in love. Couldn't get enough. Wanted the nation's supply and was willing to pay top dollar for it, which he did. The night before he was to return to the States, however, he learned that he couldn't take the beloved delicacy, which he had bought copious amounts of, on the flight home. Some kind of unfair and damn outrageous FAA rule prohibited it. Undaunted, Booker spent half the night trying to figure out ways to smuggle his supply, which was packaged in unmarked tin cans, past security agents. Initially he tried to forge phony labels for the foie gras, scrawling *baked beans* or *diced carrots* on the labels with a Sharpie. Realizing that these cans with strange, handwritten English words on them would probably raise suspicion rather than diminish it, he resorted to plan B: he ate half his stash in the hotel room, then wrapped the remaining cans in his underwear, which he jammed into the bottom of his suitcase.

"By God, no one is ever going to look there," he said to Annis. He was right. Booker glided through the checkpoints, his contraband undetected. When he got home, he turned unusually greedy, refusing to share his treat with anyone else.

"No one will appreciate it as much as I do," he said, sitting on the front porch swing and eating away. "Only my refined pallet will."

17

Traits and Attributes

Booker Noe served as master distiller of Jim Beam Brands (now Beam Suntory) for more than 40 years. During that time he increased production year after year, streamlined manufacturing processes, and created the Small Batch Bourbon Collection, which led to the establishment of a new category of American whiskey—super-premium bourbons.

During his tenure at Beam's Boston plant he wore a number of hats and held a variety of titles, both official and unofficial, ranging from distiller to human resource director to chief of security to purchasing head to brand innovator. He worked in a different time and era, when roles were not clearly defined and job descriptions not fully developed or adhered to. Simply put, he did what needed to be done to move the business forward.

He never took a distilling course or chemistry class, never studied engineering, and did not have a degree in business management. Rather, he worked, created, and managed by instinct and intuition, learning and improvising as he went along as he grew into his role as company and industry leader.

Through interviews with coworkers, peers, and friends, it is evident that Booker did possess a number of traits, attributes, and beliefs that aided him in this growth; traits, attributes, and beliefs that other managers and entrepreneurs should either consider developing in themselves, for their own career advancement, or looking for in the people that they hire.

These include:

Loyalty. When building and managing a team, Booker placed a priority on loyalty. He was an exceptionally loyal person and expected a commensurate amount of loyalty in return. He believed that if he stood by people, they better stand by him and give their best effort day in and day out. He could—and did—tolerate mistakes. What he could not tolerate in his employees was breaking rank, having a subversive attitude and a less-than-honest approach to him and to their jobs. Knowing the Big Man had their backs no matter what allowed people to try more things, to experiment and expand their talents and vision. By treating his employees like family, by letting them know he supported and trusted them, he ensured their best efforts. From a young age Booker intuitively knew that loyalty and trust was a two-way street, and once an honest relationship was attained, good things could and would happen.

Discipline. Despite some of his antics and escapades, Booker was a disciplined man who was rigorous in his approach to his career. For decades he showed up every day to a less-than-glamorous job, logged long hours in a cinder-block office, came in on weekends and holidays, and was religious when it came to overseeing the sometimes tedious details involved in running a distillery. Over time, the opportunity and temptation to ease back, to take his foot off the pedal and coast (especially once he was established) certainly grew, but he never yielded to it. He did the same thing day in and day out and pushed himself hard, and in the process set the bar high for his employees. He honored the many processes—some time-consuming—that were involved in the making of bourbon, and he understood that those processes, the details, must be attended to on a constant basis to ensure a smooth course and a consistent product. There were no short cuts in his business, only hard work—and Booker embraced that work.

Listening. To say that Booker was self-taught is not entirely accurate. Despite his penchant for talking, he knew when to keep his mouth shut and his eyes (and ears) open. He spent time listening to, and ultimately learning from, first his grandfather and later his Uncle Jere and Cousin Carl. He respected their knowledge and their experience and soaked up what they could tell him. He wasn't afraid to ask questions of not only his superiors, but also his peers, employees, suppliers, and even competitors. He was curious about what people knew and thought, and regularly sought out opinions, recommendations, and varied perspectives, all in an effort to improve and build his own knowledge and skill set. Booker regarded the ability to listen and focus as critical tools in his education. As he got older and was in a better position to teach, he would look for that same trait in his employees.

Passion. Passion was a key to Booker's long and successful run as a distiller. He was born with a passion for life—embracing all that it could offer. He carried this passion over into his job, where it manifested itself in his limitless curiosity about how things worked—and how things could work better. He loved what he did and took immense pride in how he did it. Unfortunately, passion cannot be taught. Fortunately, Booker chose a career that he fell in love with. He loved being a distiller, loved the art and science of making whiskey, and loved sharing his knowledge and experience. As an ambassador, his passion was infectious. He introduced his bourbons to people around the world with such excitement and conviction that more often than not they were turned into converts for life.

Humor. Booker loved to have a good time. Whether he was fishing, hunting, putting up hams, logging long hours at the distillery, or having a business lunch with a reporter, a party of some kind was always on the verge of breaking out. He was eager to have a laugh, get people involved in his schemes, and play pranks (or more importantly, laugh about pranks that were played on him). He worked hard, but he played just as hard, and his playful spirit was critical to building and maintaining morale and teamwork. He understood that what they were doing at the distillery, while important, wasn't life or death. Consequently, his men enjoyed working for him and appreciated his efforts to inject a certain level of levity into the job. His sense of humor broke down walls and ultimately made him approachable. His team felt that they could go to him with problems, issues, and most importantly, ideas.

Innovation. At his core, Booker was an innovator. He had a penchant for seeing things differently, a desire and talent to create. He hated the status quo (what he called monotony), choosing instead to challenge himself and those around him to stretch themselves by imagining new products, new processes, and different directions. He understood that standing pat and becoming complacent was not only boring and unfulfilling, but also dangerous. Complacency opens doors to the competition and was something to guard against. When Booker created his own bourbon and then later the Small Batch Bourbon Collection, Jim Beam Brands was on solid footing. But solid sales were not enough for Booker. He wanted more, and ultimately he got it by seeing things others did not see and trying things others would not try. And the company (and to a large degree, the entire industry) benefited.

Humility. Despite his cult-like status and the media coverage he received later in life, Booker never thought he was anyone special. Just a working man doing his job. I'm not curing cancer here, just making liquor, he was heard to say. Despite the attention he and his bourbons received, he continued to regard himself simply as another link in the long chain of Beams, doing what he was supposed to do. He never expected, wanted, or needed any special attention. Never sought out the spotlight. By being who he was, the spotlight found him, but he would have been fine if it hadn't. Throughout his life, he remained true to his roots and his work, never developed an ego, and never let things distract him. Humility came naturally to him and he expected and appreciated it in others, too. He once commented that people with big heads are big headaches, and that he'd rather not spend any time with them if he could help it. This lack of pretentiousness kept him focused on his passion and priority: making the best-tasting whiskey he could.

Respect for the competition. Rather than dismiss, critique, or ignore his competitors, Booker instead chose to learn from, study, and respect them. This attitude might be unique to his industry—many of the great distilling families, such as the Beams and the Samuels, go back generations together—but Booker took this respect to new heights. He considered other distillers his friends (and in the case of Parker Beam, the master distiller at Heaven Hill, more than that; Park was family). And rather than competing with them, he traded stories, ideas, and techniques. More than once he helped them out with an issue or a problem, and more than once they returned the favor. When Heaven Hill had a disastrous fire in 1996, Booker didn't hesitate to help Park, providing equipment and other materials to help keep his bourbon flowing.

Over the years, Booker realized that his competitors were a source of not only support, but inspiration and knowledge as well. Let the battles be fought by the sales team, he thought. To a degree, we can all learn and help each other, and in the process grow the together.

Respect for the past. As a sixth-generation distiller with family roots that stretched back centuries, Booker understood the important role his ancestors played in shaping the success of Jim Beam. Rather than eschew the old ways, he embraced them, taking what he could from his grandfathers and cousins to move the business forward. Booker's Bourbon is a reflection of that respect, a culmination of generations of experience and knowledge. More than most, Booker recognized that while the future is critical, respecting and learning from the past is equally so.

Sunset

Booker kept up a steady stream of travel throughout the nineties, diligently working his way through airports and dutifully signing autographs, posing for pictures and keeping late hours at restaurants, bars, and industry events. When he got home to Bardstown, he'd tend his garden, feed his fish, and spend time with little Freddie, his grandson.

He thought the sun rose and set on Freddie, whom he sometimes referred to as Little Book. Whenever he could he went to his football games, shouting his support for his only grandson, who just happened to be the quarterback. Before one big game, Booker took Freddie's offensive line aside and gave them a pep talk. As Booker knew, food could be a very motivating tool.

"You keep the defense off Freddie, and I'll buy you all the pizza you can eat! Soda too."

The offensive linemen jumped up and down, hooting their excitement. They then proceeded to go out and allow Freddie to get sacked a record eight times.

"You know something?" Booker said to a shell shocked and very sore Freddie after the game. "Their mommas can make them dinner tonight."

When football season was over, Booker turned his attention to basketball—religion in Kentucky. In addition to attending just about every one of Freddie's games, he erected a basketball hoop inside a shed in his backyard, complete with a free-throw line that he personally painted so Freddie could practice all he wanted.

"You got to learn how to dribble with your left hand and your right one!" Booker would yell from a stool in the corner while feeding Freddie balls. "Now do it again. No one gets better without practice! One more time now!"

Between Freddie and his other pursuits, he still made it a point to oversee the production of Booker's, still approved every batch before bottling, and still went down to the distillery to check on the other small-batch bourbons, shoot the breeze with his boys, walk the dark rack houses, and breathe the sweet, mash-filled air.

He also was still innovating. In 1999 he introduced yet another expression: very old bourbon finished in cognac barrels. He and master blender Alain Royer, founder of A. de Fussigny, had come up with the idea upon meeting and had agreed to work together. The result was the exceptional Distiller's Masterpiece, the world's first luxury bourbon, a rare and flavorful whiskey that had a limited but successful run early in the new millennium. Booker followed this initial expression up with a different version two years later: bourbon finished in port casks. (A third version—bourbon aged in sherry casks—would be introduced in 2013.) These products were proof that as the Big Man got older, the creative juices continued to flow.

His trips to the distillery, fishing at his favorite spots with Freddie and Fred, the company of his friends, Annis's home-cooked meals, and the shade of his front porch made it harder and harder for him to get back on the road. He was on the wrong side of 70, and he now felt every mile. Doing what he was doing—well, it was a younger man's game, he thought. Finally, in 2001, he told his son Fred that he'd had enough.

"I'm tired and I'm done," he said.

They were sitting out back by the fish pond, and Fred thought he'd misheard him and was confused. He, like pretty much everyone else, thought Booker was indefatigable. "What do you mean, you're done?"

"You're taking over. My time is over. I just got back from Austin. That was my last stop."

"You serious about this?"

"Hell, yeah. You ready?"

"Yes, sir. I am."

Fred was more than ready. For years he had been paying his dues, working the distillery, learning the business from every angle. Booker had been hard on him, making him earn things. At times their relationship, like many father and son relationships, had been strained, but they had persevered, worked through the tough patches, and arrived at a good place. Over the years Fred had earned the respect of his father. Booker announcing his full retirement was proof of that. The torch was passing. Generation six, say hello to generation seven. Fred had earned his stripes.

"You sure on this?" Fred asked one last time.

"I'm sure."

"All right, then."

"All right, then."

Booker left Fred and Jim Beam Brands (and the entire bourbon industry, for that matter) in good shape. The Small Batch Bourbon Collection had played a crucial role in turning the fortunes of bourbon around. Sales of Booker's, Baker's, Basil Hayden's, and most notably, Knob Creek, were soaring, growing by double-digit percentages year after year. Even premium brands such as Jim Beam Original were doing better. Bourbon had been successfully recast. Elevated. It now had status and cachet; was on a par with single-malt scotch and expensive wines. People were now coming down to Kentucky to visit the distilleries, learn the history, sip the whiskey, and engage in the bourbon experience. In 1995, in honor of the company's 200th anniversary, Beam invested significant money and time into redesigning the Clermont plant and making it more tourist friendly. (As part of its anniversary celebration, Jim Beam Brands made a rare label change on its iconic bottle of Jim Beam Bourbon, adding Booker's likeness to the label alongside those of his beloved Uncle Jere and Granddaddy Jim). The money spent on the distillery was money well spent. People liked what they saw and started to spread the word about the Beam distillery, as well as the other distilleries in the area. It's kind of like Napa Valley, except they serve ham, people said. More than worth a trip.

After Fred hit the road, first under the title of global bourbon ambassador and later as master distiller, Booker felt he could truly take it easy. He had more time for Freddie's games, more time to argue and debate with friends such as Jack Kelly, more time for dinners at home with Annis and trips to Toogie's restaurant, and more time at his favorite fishing hole on the distillery grounds.

What he liked to do most, though, was simply sit on the front porch of the Beam house and watch the world drive by while sipping on a glass of bourbon-flavored water (Kentucky Tea, he called it.) When they saw the Big Man, passersby in cars and trucks would slow down and shout out greetings.

"Love your bourbon!"

"Keep rocking, Booker!"

"Jim Beam forever!"

Booker would smile, wave, and sip on that tea, content.

"Been lucky," he told a good friend. "Been lucky."

He still sat in on tastings in his big backyard, though mostly he let Fred conduct them. Watching his son lead visitors and the media through a sampling, and hearing Fred talk about the family history with great passion pleased the Big Man to no end.

Fred had taken to his new role better than hoped for. As an ambassador he soon became highly regarded, as impactful and entertaining as Booker. His presentation skills and his innate ability to connect with consumers were second to none. Quick on his feet and able to connect with a younger audience than Booker, he won people over in convincing fashion, turning casual fans of bourbon into lifelong loyalists. What's more, he could cover two or three times the ground his father had. When he returned to Bardstown, Booker would quiz him on his travels, asking him where he went, what he said, and who he saw. With every trip Booker could see Fred's confidence grow; could see that he was a more than suitable replacement for him.

"You done good," he told Fred. "You're keeping the link strong."

His family was doing well, his brands were growing, and his status as the elder statesman of bourbon was secure. His legacy was ensured. His hobbies were keeping him busy. All was good in the Big Man's life.

Unfortunately, this state of well-being, this warm and happy sunset, didn't last as long as it should have. Soon after he was fully retired, Booker began to get sick.

*   *   *

It started with a routine eye examination. The doctor detected something he didn't like and told Booker he needed some tests. When those tests came back, diabetes was the diagnosis.

"Well, I'll be damned," Booker said. "Sooner or later, something was going to get me."

At first it was manageable. Pills every day, then shots at home. Still plenty of time to fish, play poker with the boys, go to another game of Freddie's, entertain some VIPs in his backyard. But things went steadily downhill and eventually the going got tough. Dialysis was needed. Three times a week, four hours a day at a Louisville hospital. Son Fred took off work and shuttled him back and forth. Long waits at the hospital, special diets, limited-to-no whiskey.

Booker did the best he could and made the most of it. He quickly made friends at the hospital, regaling other patients with stories as they waited for dialysis. Having his son there next to him, in the car, at the hospital, and living right next door with his wife, Sandy, helped. But, try as he might, things just weren't the same. This wasn't a life, it was just living. Nothing more. And just living, just hanging on, was something Booker Noe didn't do well.

"Just waiting, is all I'm doing," he told a good friend. "And waiting is plain monotonous."

He turned a bit more pensive and had long talks with Fred in the rides back and forth to the hospital, talks about bourbon, the responsibilities that came with being a Beam, and about being a good father to Freddie. ("Don't be as hard on him as I was on you. Learn from my mistakes.") He told Fred he was proud of him; told him that he loved him. Told him that he done good and to keep it up.

"A lot of eyes are on you," he said.

The doctor grew pessimistic, and after a checkup in early February of 2004 he told Booker the news that everyone feared: the dialysis wasn't working well enough and he was going to have to lose a foot, maybe half a leg.

Booker was quiet when he heard the news. "By losing it, I assume you mean amputation," he finally said.

"Yes."

"Would that be it? The one foot?"

"For now. We may have to amputate the other one too, down the road. We'd have to wait and see."

"Wait and see," Booker said. He sat in the chair in the doctor's office and fell quiet for a long while. Then he said, "You know, I don't think I'm going to do that. I think I'd like to go out with all the same parts I came in with." He next told the doctor that he wasn't coming back for any more dialysis, either.

"You're a good doctor and I appreciate your advice and everything you've done, but that's it, I'm through with all of that. No more machines, no more doctor visits. Cancel everything. I'm sick and tired of being sick and tired."

"Booker, if you discontinue the treatment, you'll die," the doctor said.

"How long would that take?"

"A week, maybe two."

"Then I better get going. Fred, where's my hat?"

On the way home, Fred asked his father if he was sure about his decision.

"I'm about as sure of that as I've been of anything."

"You're only 74. You still got some years left. Good years."

"Good years?" Booker asked. Then he said, "You know, life's not about quantity, it's about quality. I've lived a quality life, that's all that mattered. Don't care how long I live, never have. It's been *how* I lived. That's the important thing. And I have lived a good life, no doubt about that. Filled every damn minute up. Did what I wanted. Married the right woman, had the right job, lived in the right place, had the right boy. How many people can say that? Hell, I've been lucky, damn lucky. I can't complain, so I won't."

"Well, I guess it's your call."

"Damn right it's my call. Let's get back now, I got things to attend to."

When Booker got home, he got busy dying. Word quickly spread, and people from all over came by to pay their respects. Every night there was someone over, sitting at the kitchen table, sharing one more story, having one more drink. (Booker passed on the drink part.) While he got tired and "swimmy headed," he was, for the most part, still Booker; he still held court with authority and humor, and this put people at ease as they chatted and reminisced away.

"Hell," Jack Kelly said after another evening at Booker's house, "leave it to Booker Noe to be alive at his own wake." Two nights later, after another small party around the kitchen table had concluded, Kelly commented, "The way he's carrying on, I don't think he's ever going to die."

Booker knew otherwise and began preparations for his own funeral. He opted against the cypress casket and instead decided to be cremated and have his remains put in a special box made of cypress from an old fermenting tank. He then called up some friends who were carpenters, and they built the box along Booker's specifications.

"Make sure it's big enough for my lucky hat and a bottle of Booker's," he said.

When the men showed up, they had tears in their eyes as they presented it to him. Booker propped himself up in bed and carefully studied the box, making sure it was perfect. Satisfied, he offered the men a drink.

"Nice job, boys," he said. "I'll be proud to spend eternity in there."

Booker had a few final talks with Fred, telling him how to handle his estate, as well as how to handle the bourbon.

"Make sure they don't mess it up," he said. "Especially Booker's. It's got my name on it. Keep an eye on that whiskey."

Fred, who was by then overseeing the production of Booker's and the other small-batch bourbons, assured him that he would.

"I'll make sure it stays as good as ever," he said.

"Counting on you."

"I know that. And I won't let you down."

A week later, on February 24, Frederick Booker Noe II passed away quietly in his sleep in the very same bed his grandfather Jim Beam had died in, a life fully lived.

Half of Kentucky came to his memorial service, held at the Basilica of Saint Joseph in Bardstown on an unseasonably warm and bright midwinter day.

Afterward there was a large party, one probably more fitting for a wedding or anniversary than a funeral. Booker would have loved to have attended. Hundreds of people were there, all with a story to share, a Booker experience to recall, a toast to make. Everyone agreed: the Big Man was gone, but he would never be forgotten.

While Booker will be remembered in a number of ways, he was first and foremost a distiller. Making bourbon was his art and his passion. He played a critical role in the creation of an entire whiskey category, super-premium bourbon, and in the process helped save the spirit that defined him and his family.

But what he mostly is remembered for is his outsized personality, his generous and eager embrace of life. In too many ways to count, he was an American Original, a character whose largeness continues to be celebrated and cherished years after his passing.

At his memorial service a close family friend gave his eulogy, closing with an emotional and accurate summary of the Big Man's life:

> . . . *Booker made bourbon. That's what his grandfather did, and his father before that and his father before that and his father before that. It's what he was meant to do, what he'll be*

remembered for. He was, for the most part, self-educated when it came to whiskey making. He never took a chemistry class, didn't know much about osmosis, didn't spend much time behind a computer.

He was an instinctual craftsman and a country scientist. He understood the rhythm of bourbon-making and he respected the magic and mystery that surrounds it.

Can you imagine Booker doing anything but making bourbon?

Can you imagine Booker living anywhere else but Kentucky?

Of course not. Booker was meant to do this job. Booker was meant to live the life he led, be the man he was.

As Booker grew older, he mellowed like a good whiskey. He was proud of his son Fred, his family, the success of Jim Beam Brands, and his own Booker's bourbon, uncut, just like him. He died knowing his legacy was secured.

As we mourn his passing, there is talk of building a statue, starting a foundation, or renaming a road to honor his memory. All good things. I'd like to add to that list, though.

I think the first thing we have to do is go to the distillery, roll out a barrel of Booker's from the fifth floor, knock out the bung, and open that barrel up. Let it breathe for a while, let the bourbon mingle with the air, let it evaporate, float up into the sky, past the clouds. Let it float all the way into heaven.

Now that Booker's gone, we have to double the angel's share. We have one big angel up there, and I imagine he's pretty thirsty.

EPILOGUE

S ince Booker Noe's death in 2004, the bourbon industry has experienced explosive growth. In 2015, sales of bourbon and American whiskey were up close to 8 percent. Interest in America's native spirit is soaring. In 2015 more than 900,000 people visited what is now referred to as the Bourbon Trail in Kentucky, and dozens of new bourbon-themed restaurants, bars, and hotels have opened up throughout the Commonwealth to accommodate their growing numbers.

The bourbon boom has sparked significant growth in smaller distilleries. Seemingly daily, a new micro- or craft distillery opens its doors to an insatiable public clamoring for all things bourbon. These distilleries are no longer confined to Kentucky. The prospect of bourbon being made anywhere but the Bluegrass State, once unimaginable, is now a reality, with small distilleries sprouting up across the country in cities and states such as Chicago, San Francisco, Denver, and New York.

At the forefront of this growth remains Beam Suntory. The third-ranking spirits company worldwide, it now produces more than half of the world's bourbon. In 2015 the company listed more than 20 different bourbons.

Booker would be proud, both of Beam Suntory and the industry. That the innovation he cherished is so alive and well is a testament to his vision and his love of bourbon. While the Boston distillery has been renamed the Booker Noe Plant, and a statue of him was erected at the Clermont distillery in 2005, it is this innovation that is his true legacy.

His son, Fred, a member of the Bourbon Hall of Fame, helped pay homage to this legacy in 2014 when he introduced Booker's 25th Anniversary Bourbon, a limited-edition bottling of the very last barrels Booker ever laid down. In addition, Fred and Freddie (Little Book), who now works at the distillery, have further honored Booker's memory and spirit of innovation by overseeing the production and market introduction of a variety of bourbons and American whiskies, including Knob Creek Rye, Knob Creek Single Barrel Reserve, Jim Beam Devil's Cut and Jim Beam Single Barrel, and Booker's Rye, which was released in a limited batch in 2016. Fred also made the bold decision to release the first flavored bourbon, Red Stag, in 2009, which effectively brought in scores of new whiskey drinkers. In every new brand, every new visitor to the Bourbon Trail, and every new consumer of bourbon, Booker lives on.

By God, the party, it's just getting started!

AUTHOR'S NOTE AND ACKNOWLEDGMENTS

I traveled with Booker Noe for 10 years, crisscrossing the country with him and serving as his public relations counsel and warm-up act at countless bourbon tastings. I also had the pleasure and the privilege of being personal valet ("Jim, where are my shoes? I think I might need them tonight."); confidant ("I don't really like wine, but I drink it to be polite when I'm with other people who do."); co-conspirator ("See that salesman over there? I'm going to pretend I'm asleep if he comes over. Tell him I'm not to be disturbed."); and ultimately, I think, or would like to believe, his friend. As a writer and a novelist, I could not have made Booker up. He was, as I've frequently referred to him in this book, an American Original. Every visit I had with him—every meal, every trip, every call—was a special experience. I never knew what was going to come out of his mouth or what he was going to do next. It was exciting, and at times frightening.

The work wasn't always easy. Sometimes after media interviews, once Booker had departed, I was forced to circle back to the reporter to clarify, explain, and reposition his comments. (One time in Cleveland, recognizing that I was out of options, I simply fell on my sword in front of the columnist by saying, "If you print what he said, I will be fired.")

Situations like that notwithstanding, it was a wonderful 10 years, and I wouldn't have traded away a single minute. I knew I was lucky to work with him, knew that down the road I would recall the experience with great humor and fondness.

Talking to Booker's surviving friends and relatives to compile this book, recreating scenes and dialogue, brought the Big Man back to life for a while and made me realize all over again how lucky I was to have known him.

Some of those people included: Fred Noe, his son and seventh-generation distiller; Freddie Noe (Little Book), his grandson; Baker Beam, his low-key and rock-solid cousin; Annis, his beloved wife of 48 years; Bob Noe Hayden, his cousin; Jerry Noe, his younger brother; Jim Beam Noe, his distilling nephew; Johnny Hibbs and Jerry Summers, longtime Beam associates; Mike Donohoe and Tom Maas, former Beam executives and good friends; Kathleen DiBenedetto, a favorite of Booker's; Bill Samuels Jr., longtime family friend and bourbon peer; Kevin Smith, Dan Cohen, and Paula Erickson, current Beam executives; Marilyn "Toogie" Dick and Jack Kelley, the core of his inner circle; and Jerry Grider, his nephew. All of them—and others—contributed their time and memories to make this book possible. Thank you!

JIM BEAN'S CURRENT BOURBON LINEUP

Jim Beam Bourbon

Jim Beam Black

Knob Creek

Knob Creek Rye

Knob Creek Single Barrel
Reserve

Basil Hayden's

Baker's

Booker's

Old Grand-Dad

Old Crow

Jim Beam Devil's Cut

Booker's Rye

Red Stag Black Cherry

Jim Beam Apple

Jim Beam Honey

Jim Beam Distiller's
Masterpiece

Jim Beam Bonded

Jim Beam Rye

Jim Beam Single Barrel

Jim Beam Signature Craft

Jim Beam Harvest Bourbon
Collection

Jim Beam Kentucky Fire*

Jim Beam Double Oak*

Jim Beam Maple*

Knob Creek Smoked Maple*

Knob Creek 2001 Limited
Edition

* Kentucky Straight Bourbon with Natural Flavors.

FAVORITE BOOKER QUOTES

"I know bourbon gets better with age, because the older I get, the more I like it."

"A respectable amount of bourbon to pour in a glass is about two fingers. Lucky for me, I have big fingers."

"Outlawing alcohol was the dumbest thing the government ever did. People aren't going to go without their toddies and their pick-me-ups."

"It takes years to make our whiskey. Fortunately, it doesn't take me long to drink it."

"The party, it's just getting started!"

"By God . . . [fill in the blank]"

"Be good now!"

"Hell, I'd live in a rack house if they let me."

"Let me think on that."

"Tasting Booker's is like tasting the past."

BOURBON GLOSSARY

beer well Holding tank where the fermented mash sits until it is distilled.

bonded bourbon whiskey Bourbon whiskey that has been aged and bottled according to the Bottled-in-Bond Act of 1897. It is straight bourbon whiskey, made at one time and in one location for at least four years, then bottled at 100 proof.

bourbon whiskey Made in the United States from a fermented mash containing at least 51 percent corn. It must be produced at no more than 160 proof, aged in new American oak charred barrels at no more than 125 proof, and bottled at no less than 80 proof.

doubler A smaller, pot-style still in which whiskey is distilled a second time to improve its quality. It is some-times called a thumper because of the sound it used to make.

fermenters Large vats or tanks that house the mash. Yeast is added to the mash while it's in the fermenters, converting the sugars into alcohol. A beer-like liquid is produced in these vats, which used to be made of cypress, but are now mostly stainless steel.

mash cooker Tank where the corn/rye mixture is cooked and the malted barley is added. The malted barley releases an enzyme that converts grain starch into sugars. When the conversion is complete, the mash is transferred to fermenters.

moonshine Distilled spirits produced in an unlicensed, unregulated still without payment of taxes, and hence illegal. Seldom aged and produced from anything that will ferment, moonshine (made at night, when the moon is shining) is often a health hazard.

proof A statement of alcohol content. Proof is two times the percentage of alcohol by volume. In other words, 100-proof whiskey is 50 percent alcohol by volume.

sour mash A process developed by Dr. James C. Crow around 1840 to provide uniformity in bourbon production. A portion of the previous days' mash is added to new mash to ensure consistent quality and character.

still An apparatus, usually made of copper, in which distiller's beer is purified by means of heating the liquid to at least 176 degrees but less than 212 degrees Fahrenheit.

Because alcohol boils at a temperature lower than water, alcohol can be evaporated, collected, and condensed.

white dog   Unaged distillate. Also known as green whiskey or high wine, it is colorless.

FAVORITE FOOD AND COCKTAIL RECIPES

Booker enjoyed eating and drinking. Some of his and his family's favorite dishes and cocktail recipes follow.

COCKTAILS

Whiskey Sour

Ingredients

1½ parts Jim Beam Bourbon

1 part lemon juice

½ teaspoon sugar

1 lemon or orange wedge

1 cherry

Instructions

1. Add the sugar and the bourbon to the lemon juice.
2. Garnish with lemon or orange wedge and cherry.

Classic Old Fashioned

Ingredients

1$\frac{1}{2}$ parts Knob Creek Bourbon

3 dashes Angostura bitters

Pinch of raw sugar

1 cherry

Instructions

1. Muddle sugar and bitters in a rocks glass.
2. Add bourbon and ice.
3. Stir.
4. Top with cherry as garnish.

Mint Old Fashioned

Ingredients

2 parts Knob Creek Bourbon

2 teaspoons simple syrup

3–4 dashes aromatic bitters

8–10 mint leaves

1 mint sprig

1 orange twist

Instructions

1. Muddle simple syrup, bitters, and mint leaves in an old-fashioned glass.
2. Pour bourbon into the glass and add a large piece of ice.
3. Stir until drink is cold and ingredients are mixed.
4. Garnish with mint sprig and orange twist.

Maple Hot Toddy

Ingredients

$1\frac{1}{2}$ parts Knob Creek Smoked Maple Bourbon

$\frac{1}{2}$ part honey

$\frac{1}{2}$ cup hot water

$\frac{1}{2}$ part fresh lemon juice

1 cinnamon stick

1 lemon wedge

Instructions

1. Combine bourbon, honey, hot water, and lemon juice.
2. Stir.
3. Garnish with cinnamon stick and lemon wedge.

Booker Noe's Mint Julep

Ingredients

1½ parts Booker's Bourbon
Crushed ice
½ tablespoon mint syrup (recipe follows)
1 mint sprig

Instructions

1. Fill julep glass with crushed ice.
2. Add mint syrup and Booker's Bourbon
3. Garnish with mint sprig.

Mint Syrup Recipe

1. Boil 1 cup water and 1 cup sugar for 5 minutes. Do not stir. Cool.
2. Fill 1-quart jar to the top with mint leaves.
3. Pour syrup over mint, cap jar tightly, and refrigerate for 24 hours.
4. Discard mint.
5. Keep syrup refrigerated.

Recipe makes enough syrup for 10 drinks.

Classic Manhattan

Ingredients

2 parts Knob Creek Rye Whiskey

$\frac{1}{2}$ part sweet vermouth

2–3 dashes Angostura bitters

1 maraschino cherry

Instructions

1. Pour whiskey, sweet vermouth, and bitters into a shaker filled with ice.
2. Stir until outside of shaker is very cold to the touch.
3. Place ice and maraschino cherry in a rocks glass.
4. Strain the contents of the shaker into the glass.

BBG (Beam Black and Ginger Ale)

Ingredients

$1\frac{1}{2}$ parts Jim Beam Black Bourbon

2 dashes bitters

4 parts ginger ale

1 lemon wedge

Instructions

1. Combine bourbon and bitters in shaker with no ice and shake vigorously.
2. Pour into a glass filled with ice and top with ginger ale.
3. Garnish with a lemon wedge.

Front Porch Peach Tea

Ingredients

$1\frac{1}{4}$ parts Jim Beam Black Bourbon

$\frac{3}{4}$ part DeKuyper Peachtree Schnapps Liqueur

4 parts iced tea

1 peach wedge

Instructions

1. Build bourbon, schnapps, and iced tea in order listed over ice in a tall highball glass.
2. Garnish with peach wedge.

Knob Creek and Ginger Beer

Ingredients

$1\frac{1}{2}$ parts Knob Creek Bourbon

4 parts ginger beer

$\frac{1}{2}$ part fresh lime juice

1 lime wedge

Instructions

1. Fill glass with ice, fresh lime juice, and bourbon.
2. Top with ginger beer.
3. Garnish with lime wedge.

Cut and Cola

Ingredients

1 part Jim Beam Devil's Cut Bourbon

3 parts cola

1 lime twist

Instructions

1. Add bourbon and cola to a tall highball glass filled with ice.
2. Garnish with lime twist.

Kentucky Mule

Ingredients

2 parts Jim Beam Black Bourbon

3 parts ginger beer

1 splash lime juice

1 lime wheel

Instructions

1. Build bourbon, ginger beer, and lime juice over ice in a tall highball glass.
2. Garnish with lime wheel.

Kentucky Bourbon Margarita

Ingredients

1 part Jim Beam Bourbon

Splash of triple sec

Splash of sweet-and-sour mix

1 lime wedge

Salt (optional)

Instructions

1. Salt rim of glass if desired.
2. Blend bourbon, triple sec, and sweet-and-sour mix together and shake well.
3. Pour over ice and garnish with a lime wedge.

Or simply combine Jim Beam Bourbon with a favorite margarita mix.

APPETIZERS

Booker's Beaten Biscuits

6 cups all-purpose flour

1 cup lard

1 teaspoon salt

2 tablespoons sugar

$\frac{1}{2}$ teaspoon baking powder

1 cup whole milk

Take 6 cups of all-purpose flour and cut in 1 cup of lard. Make *double sure* lard is cut in until it is mealy (no large pieces of lard). Add 1 teaspoon of salt, 2 tablespoons of sugar, and $\frac{1}{2}$ teaspoon of baking powder. Mix thoroughly. Add 1 cup of whole milk. Run through a dough break until dough is smooth. Roll out until dough is about $\frac{3}{8}$ of an inch thick. Cut biscuits with a small cutter. Punch holes with a folk, 3 times each. Make sure the holes are completely through the biscuits. Bake at 300 degrees for about 1 hour, or until brown.

Makes about 5 dozen biscuits.

Great with thinly sliced country ham!

Jim Beam Bourbon Barbecue Drumsticks

Ingredients

$\frac{1}{2}$ cup Jim Beam Bourbon

$\frac{1}{2}$ cup teriyaki sauce

1 cup oyster sauce

$\frac{1}{4}$ cup soy sauce

$\frac{1}{4}$ cup ketchup

2 tablespoons garlic powder

2 dashes liquid smoke flavoring

$\frac{1}{2}$ cup white sugar

$1\frac{1}{2}$ pounds chicken wings, separated at joints, tips discarded

$\frac{1}{4}$ cup honey

Preparation

In a large bowl, mix all ingredients except the chicken wings and the honey. Place wings in the bowl, cover, and marinate in the refrigerator 8 hours, or overnight. Preheat the grill for low heat. Lightly oil the grill grate. Arrange chicken on the grill and discard the marinade. Grill wings on one side for 20 minutes, then turn and brush with honey. Continue grilling for 25 minutes more, or until juices run clear.

Stuffed Mushrooms with Jim Beam Bourbon

Ingredients

24 medium-sized mushrooms

1 cup melted butter

2 small onions, minced

3 cloves garlic, minced

$\frac{1}{2}$ cup parsley, minced

2 tablespoons flour

$\frac{1}{2}$ cup seasoned bread crumbs

1 cup sour cream

Salt and pepper, to taste

Jim Beam Bourbon

Parmesan cheese

Preparation

Remove and chop mushroom stems. Combine chopped stems with butter, onion, garlic, and parsley. Mix well. Add flour, bread crumbs, sour cream, and salt and pepper. Mix well. Arrange mushroom caps hollow side up in a shallow baking dish, and drizzle a small amount of Jim Beam Bourbon in each cap. Fill caps with stuffing, then sprinkle with parmesan cheese to taste. Add enough bourbon to baking dish to cover the bottom. Bake for 20 minutes in a 375-degree oven.

SIDES

Kentucky Bourbon Baked Beans

Ingredients

$\frac{1}{4}$ cup Jim Beam Bourbon

2 28-ounce cans baked beans

$\frac{1}{2}$ cup chili sauce

$\frac{1}{2}$ cup strong coffee (best if left over from the morning)

3 teaspoons dry mustard

Preparation

Combine all ingredients. Pour into a 2-quart casserole dish. Bake at 350 degrees for 1 hour, or until good and bubbly.

Tarragon Snap Peas with Basil Hayden's Bourbon

Ingredients

Basil Hayden's Bourbon

8 cups boiling water

2 pounds snap peas

2 tablespoons chopped fresh tarragon

2 tablespoons olive oil

Preparation

Blanch peas for 1 minute in boiling water. Cool under cold running water. Transfer to wok or skillet and stir-fry in olive oil and tarragon for 2–3 minutes, stirring frequently. Drizzle with Basil Hayden's.

Serves 6.

Knob Creek Bourbon-Rosemary String Beans

Ingredients

2 tablespoons Knob Creek Bourbon

2 quarts salted water

3 tablespoons dried rosemary, tied in a piece of cheesecloth

2 pounds string beans, tips and stems removed

Unsalted butter (optional)

Salt to taste (optional)

Preparation

Bring salted water to boil and add the rosemary. Simmer for 15 minutes, then add the beans and boil slowly for 15–20 minutes, depending on how tender you like them. Top each serving with a drizzle of Knob Creek, and a dab of butter and sprinkle of salt if desired.

Serves 6.

ENTRÉES

Knob Creek Smoked Maple Bourbon Glazed Ham

Ingredients

10–12 pound, bone-in, fully cooked ham

1 cup water

2 cups Knob Creek Smoked Maple Bourbon

$\frac{1}{4}$ cup Dijon mustard

$1\frac{1}{2}$ cups brown sugar

$\frac{1}{2}$ cup honey

$\frac{1}{2}$ cup apple cider vinegar

1 cinnamon stick

Juice of 1 orange

$\frac{1}{2}$ teaspoon salt

Preparation

Preheat oven to 275 degrees. Place ham in a roasting pan; add 1 cup of water to the bottom of the pan. Cover with foil and place in the oven to warm through, about 2 hours. Begin making glaze (recipe follows). After about 2 hours, your ham should be warmed through. Remove it from the oven and remove the foil. Turn the oven up to 375 degrees. Pour the glaze over the ham and place the ham back in the oven, uncovered, for another 10–15 minutes, until the glaze becomes sticky on the outside of the ham and starts to caramelize. Remove from oven, slice, and enjoy.

Glaze Preparation

Heat a large, heavy-bottomed saucepan over medium heat and combine the Knob Creek Smoked Maple bourbon, mustard, brown sugar, honey, cider vinegar, and cinnamon stick. As the mixture comes to a gentle boil, whisk to dissolve the sugars. Lower the heat to medium-low and continue to cook and reduce liquid. Whisk the mixture occasionally until it begins to thicken, about 30 minutes. After about 20 minutes, the mixture will begin to look like a glaze and the bubbles will slow down and appear smaller. Remove from heat and finish the glaze with the juice of 1 orange and $\frac{1}{2}$ teaspoon salt. Remove the cinnamon stick, then set aside.

Jim Beam Bourbon Barbecue Sauce

Ingredients

2 cups ketchup

1 cup brown sugar, packed

4 tablespoons Worcestershire sauce

2 teaspoons dry mustard

1 cup Jim Beam Bourbon

4 tablespoons cider vinegar

4 tablespoons soy sauce

$\frac{1}{2}$ teaspoon cayenne pepper

Preparation

Combine all ingredients in a medium saucepan. Bring to a boil over high heat, stirring occasionally. Reduce heat to low and simmer uncovered 20–25 minutes or until thickened, stirring occasionally.

Makes 3–4 cups.

Jim Beam Bourbon Baby Back Ribs

Ingredients

2 full racks baby back ribs, quartered

1 quart beef broth

2 cups Jim Beam Bourbon Barbecue Sauce (see recipe on page 206)

1 cup honey

Preparation

Place ribs and beef broth in a large heavy pot or Dutch oven and add enough water to fully cover the ribs. Simmer over low heat for about 1 hour. Once ribs are tender, remove and set aside. Preheat grill to medium heat. Combine barbecue sauce and honey in a medium bowl. Baste ribs generously with sauce and grill for about 4 minutes on each side, or until they reach desired degree of doneness.

Steak À La Jim Beam

Ingredients

¼ cup Jim Beam Bourbon

2 tablespoons light sesame oil

2 teaspoons Worcestershire sauce

2 1-inch thick T-bone or rib-eye steaks

Preparation

Mix first three ingredients well. Place the two steaks on a shallow dish or plate and pour the marinade over the steaks. Cover with plastic wrap and refrigerate at least 1 hour prior to grilling. After 30 minutes in the refrigerator, turn the steaks over and allow to marinate for an additional 30 minutes. When the steaks are finished marinating, place on a hot grill and cook to your satisfaction. Serve your steaks with a tossed salad, baked potatoes, hot rolls, and refreshing Jim Beam Bourbon and cola.

Bourbon-Roasted Venison with Hunter's Sauce

Ingredients

2 cups Booker's Bourbon

12-pound leg of venison

4 cloves garlic, slivered

2 cups olive oil

2 cups Worcestershire sauce

1 medium onion, sliced

5 tablespoons dried rosemary

2 tablespoons freshly ground black pepper

Hunter's Sauce (recipe follows)

Preparation

Wipe the meat with paper towels. Make deep incisions all over the roast and insert slivers of garlic. Reserve 1 cup of the olive oil, but combine all of the other remaining ingredients except the sauce. Pour marinade over meat, cover, and refrigerate for 12 hours or overnight, turning every few hours. Preheat oven to 450 degrees. Place the venison leg in a roaster with about half the marinade. Pour remaining olive oil over venison. Bake for 15 minutes uncovered. Turn heat down to 250 degrees and insert a meat thermometer into the thickest part (do not let it touch the bone). Cover with foil and bake until the thermometer reaches 150 degrees for medium (about 3 hours) or 165 degrees for well done. Baste often.

Serves 10–12.

Note: As Booker's Bourbon is bottled straight from the barrel, it is high in proof. Please take care when baking with Booker's in a gas oven, as the alcohol flash point is lower in a higher-proof spirit.

Hunter's Sauce

Ingredients

2 tablespoons unsalted butter

2 tablespoons chopped green onions (including some tops)

4 cups sliced mushrooms

Salt

$\frac{1}{2}$ teaspoon freshly ground black pepper

$\frac{1}{3}$ cup Booker's Bourbon

1 cup degreased pan drippings

1 cup peeled, seeded, and chopped fresh tomatoes

1 teaspoon cornstarch mixed with 1 teaspoon water

Preparation

In a large saucepan, melt the butter over medium heat and add the green onions, mushrooms, a pinch of salt, and the pepper. Sauté about 10 minutes, until vegetables are cooked. Add the Booker's and turn up the heat up to high. Simmer briefly. Lower the heat to medium, add the pan drippings and tomatoes, and cook about 5 minutes. Do not overcook the tomatoes; they should be slightly firm. Stir the cornstarch mixture into the sauce and cook 2 minutes more, or until thickened. Serve hot.

Makes about $3\frac{1}{2}$–4 cups.

Note: As Booker's Bourbon is bottled straight from the barrel, it is high in proof. Please take care when baking with Booker's in a gas oven, as the alcohol flash point is lower in a higher-proof spirit.

Bourbon-Flambéed Barbecued Pork Chops

Ingredients

pork chops

Jim Beam Bourbon Barbecue Sauce (see recipe on page 208)

Booker's Bourbon

Preparation

Marinate pork chops in the barbecue sauce and bake as directed. Placed finished pork chops on a glass blaze. Drizzle each pork chop with approximately 1 tbsp. of Booker's Bourbon and flambé before serving.

Pork Loin with Knobby Apples and Sweet Onions

Ingredients

Pork Loin

1 boneless pork loin roast (preferably center cut), about 3 pounds
Salt and cracked pepper to taste
2 tablespoons grainy Creole mustard
$\frac{1}{3}$ cup of honey (Tupelo is best, but clover or wildflower is fine)
$\frac{1}{4}$ teaspoon chopped fresh rosemary
Juice of $\frac{1}{4}$ lemon

Apples and Onions

1 tablespoon butter
1 tablespoon olive oil
1 large Maui or other sweet onion, peeled, halved, and sliced
2 apples (preferably Honeycrisp or Granny Smith), peeled, cored, and sliced
1 cup plus 2 ounces Knob Creek Bourbon
$\frac{1}{4}$ teaspoon chopped fresh rosemary
Juice of $\frac{1}{4}$ lemon
1 teaspoon Asian fish sauce
$\frac{1}{3}$ cup of honey (Tupelo is best, but clover or wildflower is fine)
Salt and cracked pepper to taste

Preparation

Preheat oven to 425 degrees. In a large skillet, heat butter and olive oil over medium heat. Sauté onions for 4–6 minutes, stirring (a little bit of browning is okay). Add apples and continue to cook for 5 more minutes.

In the meantime, season pork with salt and cracked pepper, then rub with grainy mustard and half of the honey. Set the pork on a rack and sprinkle with $\frac{1}{4}$ teaspoon rosemary and the juice of $\frac{1}{4}$ lemon. Line a roasting pan with foil to catch the juices. Roast the pork at 425 degrees for 10 minutes, then lower the heat to 325 degrees and cook for an additional 20 minutes. *Do not open the oven during this process!*

Five minutes before the pork is done, remove the apples from the skillet. Heat the apples in another skillet over medium-high heat, and when they start to sizzle, very carefully add 1 cup of Knob Creek bourbon and flambé. *Be careful of the alcohol flames!* After 1 minute, add the fish sauce, 2 ounces of Knob Creek Bourbon, the juice of $\frac{1}{4}$ lemon, $\frac{1}{3}$ cup honey, and $\frac{1}{4}$ teaspoon rosemary. Cook together for 2–3 minutes until the mixture has the consistency of a sauce. Add a bit of water if needed to thin the sauce a bit. Season with salt and pepper, and simmer for 30 seconds.

Remove the pork from the oven and raise the heat to 425 degrees. Arrange the apples and onions on the roast carefully, and pour $\frac{3}{4}$ of the sauce over it, saving the remaining sauce for later. Put roast back into the oven and bake at 425 degrees for 10 minutes, or until the apple-onion topping starts to get slightly browned. Remove the roast from the oven and pour the remaining sauce over it, then let it rest for 10 minutes. Slice and serve with the apples, onions, and pan sauce.

Knob Creek Bourbon Chicken

Ingredients

1 whole boneless chicken breast
1 cup flour
Small amount of cooking oil
4 ounces fresh mushrooms, quartered
Salt, pepper, and garlic powder to taste
1 cup whipping cream (do not whip)
1 tablespoon Knob Creek Bourbon
1 tablespoon beef stock

Preparation

Flour chicken breast on all sides. Sauté chicken in oil, browning well on both sides. Remove chicken from pan. Add mushrooms and sauté in pan, adding salt, pepper, and garlic powder to taste. Return chicken to pan. Pour whipping cream over chicken. Cook until cream is reduced by half, or until it becomes thickened. Add Knob Creek Bourbon and beef stock.

Bourbon Barbecued Shrimp

Ingredients

2 pounds large (16–20 count) raw shrimp, peeled and deveined

1 teaspoon fine sea salt

$\frac{1}{2}$ teaspoon freshly ground black pepper

$\frac{1}{4}$ teaspoon cayenne pepper

2 tablespoons extra-virgin olive oil

Jim Beam Bourbon Barbecue Sauce (see recipe on page 208)

Preparation

Make the barbecue sauce. This may be done a day ahead. Cool the sauce, cover, and chill. Reheat before the shrimp is added to it.

Place the shrimp in a gallon-sized plastic bag. Add the salt, black pepper, and cayenne pepper and toss to coat well.

Heat the oil over high heat in a large skillet. Sauté the shrimp, turning once, for about 5 minutes or until pink and lightly browned. Add to the hot barbecue sauce. Allow to sit for a few minutes, then serve with crusty bread.

Bourbon-Marinated Flank Steak

Ingredients

1 large flank steak (approximately 2 pounds)
1 recipe bourbon marinade (recipe follows)

Bourbon Marinade

$\frac{1}{2}$ cup light soy sauce
3 tablespoons vegetable oil
2 medium onions, sliced
3 large cloves garlic, chopped
2 tablespoons minced fresh ginger root
2 tablespoons dark brown sugar
$\frac{1}{4}$ teaspoon hot pepper sauce
$\frac{1}{2}$ cup Knob Creek Bourbon

Preparation

Trim all visible fat from the flank steak.

In a heavy-duty, gallon-sized plastic bag with a zip top, mix together all of the marinade ingredients. Add steak. Refrigerate for at least 8 hours or as long as 24 hours.

Cook on a hot grill for 8 minutes on the first side and 5 minutes on the second side for a medium-rare steak. Increase the cooking time if a more well-done steak is desired.

To serve, cut across the grain into 1-inch–wide strips.

Serves 4–6.

Note: This marinade can also be used with other cuts of steak, such as sirloin, sirloin strip, or filet. The marinating time can be cut to 6–8 hours for these tender cuts.

DESERTS

Jim Beam Bourbon Balls

Ingredients

36 pecan halves

4 tablespoons Jim Beam Bourbon

6 tablespoons butter, softened

4 cups confectioners' sugar

Jim Beam Bourbon (amount varies by preference)

$\frac{1}{2}$ pound semisweet chocolate

Preparation

Soak pecan halves in 4 tablespoons of Jim Beam Bourbon, 2 hours to overnight. Drain. Drink Jim Beam. Combine butter with confectioners' sugar. Add enough bourbon to make mixture soft enough to roll into balls. Place a pecan half in the center of each ball. Refrigerate. Drink any Jim Beam left over. When bourbon balls are solid, grate chocolate and melt it over water in a double boiler. Using a dipping tong or fork, dip each ball into the chocolate to coat. Place bourbon balls in an airtight container and store in the refrigerator.

Bread Pudding with Bourbon Sauce

Ingredients

Bread Pudding

1 loaf stale bread, cubed

4 cups milk

2 cups sugar

8 tablespoons melted butter

3 eggs

2 tablespoons vanilla

1 cup raisins

1 cup pecans

1 teaspoon nutmeg

Whiskey Sauce

$\frac{1}{2}$ cup butter

$1\frac{1}{2}$ cups powdered sugar

2 egg yolks

$\frac{1}{2}$ cup Jim Beam Bourbon

Preparation

For bread pudding: Combine all ingredients. Mixture should be very moist but not soupy. Pour into buttered 9 × 13-inch baking dish. Place in preheated 350-degree oven. Bake for approximately 1 hour and 15 minutes, until top is golden brown.

For whiskey sauce: Combine butter and sugar over medium heat until all butter is absorbed. Remove from heat and blend in egg yolks. Pour in Jim Beam Bourbon gradually, stirring constantly. Sauce will thicken as it cools. Serve warm over finished bread pudding.

Bourbon Sweet Potato and Apple Casserole

Ingredients

3 pounds sweet potatoes

3 large Granny Smith apples

6 tablespoons butter, cut into small pieces

1 teaspoon salt

1 tablespoon finely chopped crystallized ginger

$\frac{1}{4}$ cup dark brown sugar

$\frac{1}{2}$ teaspoon allspice

$\frac{1}{2}$ cup Knob Creek Bourbon

2 tablespoons chopped fresh mint leaves

Preparation

Peel and thinly slice the sweet potatoes and apples.

Place a layer of the sweet potatoes into a generously buttered 9 ✕ 13-inch shallow baking dish. Dot with $\frac{1}{3}$ of the butter and sprinkle with $\frac{1}{3}$ of the salt. Add a layer of apples, dot with $\frac{1}{3}$ of the remaining butter, and sprinkle with the remaining salt, the chopped ginger, the sugar, and the allspice. Top with the remaining potatoes and pour the bourbon over the layers. Top with the remaining butter.

Cover the pan with heavy-duty foil and bake in the center of a preheated 400-degree oven for 45 minutes. Remove from oven and carefully remove the foil. Return to the oven and bake 15–20 minutes longer, or until lightly browned.

Garnish with the chopped mint before serving.

Serves 8–10 as a side dish.

Praline Bourbon Cheesecake Squares

Ingredients

Crust

1 cup flour
¼ cup dark brown sugar, packed
1 cup finely chopped pecans
1 stick (4 ounces) butter, melted
2 tablespoons Knob Creek Bourbon

Preparation

Stir together all of the ingredients. Press into the bottom of a 9 × 13-inch baking pan. Bake for 15 minutes in a preheated 350-degree oven. Cool on a rack before adding the filling.

Filling

16 ounces cream cheese, softened
½ cup granulated sugar
½ cup light brown sugar
3 tablespoons Knob Creek Bourbon
3 large eggs

Topping

2 cups sour cream
1 teaspoon pure vanilla extract
6 tablespoons granulated sugar
36 lightly toasted pecan halves

Preparation

Cut the cheese into cubes and whip it in the food processor or with an electric mixer. Beat in the sugars. Add the bourbon and the eggs and beat until the mixture is very smooth and fluffy. Pour the filling into the cooled crust.

Return the pan to the 350-degree oven and bake for about 25 minutes, or until set and puffed.

Make the sour cream topping by gently stirring together the sour cream, vanilla, and the sugar with a whisk.

Remove from the oven and spread with the topping.

Return to the oven and bake 5 minutes longer.

Cool on a rack.

Lightly mark off into squares. Top each square with a pecan half.

Chill until very cold. When chilled through, cut into squares with a knife dipped into hot water.

Makes 3 dozen squares.

INDEX

Note: In this index, "BN" refers to Frederick Booker Noe, II.